(

The Fall of The Godfather

BY W.G. DAVIS

ISBN-13:
978-1545505922

ISBN-10:
1545505926

Foreword

By Anthony "Junior" D'Amato

John and I go way back. I met him back in the mid 50's at Franklin K. Lane High School in Brooklynn.

Back then anyone who knew John knew that he was a badass.

He hated school and he would be out more than he would be in school.

One day John, me and some of the other boys skipped school. We were just roaming the neighborhood when my uncle drove past us.

I remember that he stopped his big station wagon right in the middle of street and got out of his car and started to yell at us.

John just looked at me and said, "What the hell is his problem?"

I still remember that day as if it was just yesterday.

We had a lot of fun back then. We didn't have a care in the world.

John was never close to his father. He would just change the subject whenever the topic of his home life was brought up.

We knew that he was poor, hell; we were all poor we were from the Brooklyn.

When my mother found out that I was hanging with John and his two of his brothers, Peter and Richard, she told me to stay away from them, that they were nothing but trouble. But being with John back then was what I wanted.

I never got in any real trouble back then. Or should I say that I never got caught for some of the things that we did.

We would do some odd jobs for the mob back then. Nothing too crazy you might say. We broke some windows and harassed a few folks but nothing like murder or anything like that.

Then around 56 or sometime close to then we got more involved with the street gangs in New York.

John was part of the Fulton-Rockaway Boys, a gang named for an intersection in Brooklyn.

It didn't take John long to be considered the leader of the gang. He was promoted because he took no shit from nobody and he knew how to fight. And trust me he wasn't afraid to swing at you.

The street gang life was like living a fucking dream when you are only 17. Nobody ever told us what to do and we were the masters of our own destiny.

For the few years that we stayed in the Fulton-Rockaway Boys we did a lot of jobs for the mob. And we were eventually moved up the ranks and starting to live the life of a real mobster.

In the late 50's John is dating a girl named Victoria. They met sometime around 57 or 58. In 1961 they had their first child, Angela and before too long they had four more kids, Victoria, John Jr, Frank and Peter. Some of them were born while I was away at prison.

Then in 1962, after marrying Victoria, John tried to work a legitimate job in a coat factory and driving trucks part time, but that life was not for him.

In 1963 I was arrested and convicted of assault with a deadly weapon and attempted murder in upstate New York.

It was my first real case I ever caught so the state was a little lenient on me. I did three years in prison followed by a few years of parole.

While in prison I ran into John as I was being transferred to a prison in upstate New York. He told me to make sure that I looked him up when I got out.

I stayed clean during my parole years. Then on Tuesday April 11th, 1972 I was officially released from parole and I went straight to the old neighborhood looking for John and the guys.

I won't go into any details of what our lives were like in the 80's and 90's. But I will say that it was far more exciting than any book or television show could ever portray.

We were truly untouchable in our minds. We had money, women and everyone respected us.

Movies and books portray John as some monster. But for us that were around him we seen the side of him that the world never saw. He was a loving father and husband and he would do good things for people.

I remember on more than one occasion when he would give me an envelope to deliver to an older couple in the old neighborhood. I would knock at the door and when they answered I would hand them the envelope and tell them that John sent it.

And the look of surprise on their faces when they opened it up and found cash, that was something that I would always remember about the good side of John Gotti.

On a couple occasions I was told that they don't know why he would send them money.

A couple of times the people were hesitant about taking the money because they thought that it was a loan sharking ploy and they would have to pay it back with interest.

I would take the money back to John and tell him that the money was refused because of that fear and he would send me right back out with the message that it was a gift.

I found out later in life that when John learned that older people were having financial problems he would try to help them.

His saying was, "You always stand up for a standup guy and help him out. Because you never know when you may need some help. It's like paying it forward."

A lot of people didn't know that John would have a fourth of July party every year outside the Bergin Hunt and Fish Club in Ozone Park in Queens on 101st Avenue between 98th and 99th Street.

It was an all day long festival, with hot dogs and hamburgers. He would make sure that the kids had ice-cream and cotton candy. He even made sure that we got the big blow up things that the kids could go into and jump around. (A bounce house) And on top of it all he made sure that American flags flew from the houses on the side streets. And he even had fireworks.

Someone came up to John a few days after the party and told him that the city guessed that over 2000 people attended the block party. He just smiled and said, "Good." And he walked away.

I remember one year I had to do a few things and I got back to the club late. As I walked down 101st Avenue all I could hear is the sound of hundreds of people yelling "Gotti! Gotti! Gotti!"

He was a hero to these people; he was their version of royalty.

I still remember the day that I heard that John had died in prison. I got a phone call from Tony "The

Tiger" Joseph at around eight o'clock in the morning on June 11th 2002.

He told me that John had died from the cancer that he had in his throat. And all I could think was that this man was one of the most powerful men in New York and it is cancer that would finally take him out.

I'm 75 years old now and living a quiet life in South Florida. Sometimes I walk down to the fishing pier and look out at the water and think back on those days. I thank God that I am still alive to see my children and grandchildren grow up.

I don't miss the life of crime any more but to be honest, some days I do miss my friend John.

Prologue

The Gambino Family History

The Gambino crime family is the most publicized family of the American Mafia. It's one of "Five Families" based out of New York that dominates organized crime in the United States. The Gambino family got its name from previous boss Carlo Gambino who controlled the family from 1959 until his death in October 1976.

Carlo Gambino

The family got its start in the late 1800's as the Salvatore "Toto" D'Aquila gang of Manhattan who joined the established Morello gang. They were the first Italian American gang in New York, and possibly the entire United States.

Their reign lasted for twenty years until the matriarch of the family, Giuseppe Morello and his underboss, Ignazio Saietta, were sent to prison after a counterfeiting conviction. Realizing the gang was in rough shape; D'Aquila split away from the remaining members and formed his own gang in East Harlem.

Using his established connections with other Mafia leaders, D'Aquila's gang quickly became a powerful influence in New York.

The Early History

Salvatore "Toto" D'Aquila

Through a series of shifts of power from one gang to another, Salvatore "Toto" D'Aquila formed alliances with other Mafia bosses and took down the weaker gangs absorbing their rackets. From 1910-1917 D'Aquila established and reestablished the largest Italian gang in New York. They controlled more rackets than any other gang in the area.

Nineteen-twenty brought prohibition outlawing the sale and distribution of alcohol, and a well-paid illegal racket for the New York gangs. During this time more gangs emerged with the first gang being a spinoff of the ailing Morello gang based in the Bronx and East Harlem.

It was led by Gaetano Reina, an intelligent businessman who not only went after the unlawful sale and distribution of alcohol, but had complete control over icebox distribution in the city. His gang would later become the Lucchese Crime family one of the "Five Families" of New York.

The second gang to emerge in the 1920's was led by a fierce and powerful mobster name Joe Profaci. His gang would later become the final of the "Five Families" to be established named the Colombo crime family.

In 1920, the Morello gang had disbanded with its members leaving or joining other gangs around New York. This left D'Aquila and his only real rival Giuseppe "Joe the Boss" Masseria in control of New York. Masseria had taken over the interests of the Morello family and by late 1920 he was looking for further expansion, but D'Aquila was standing in his way.

In 1928 D'Aquila, was gunned down by Masseria murderer's leaving D'Aquila's second in command Alfred Mineo in charge of the family. It wouldn't last. In late 1930 Masseria murderers gunned down Mineo and his top lieutenant Steve Ferrigno, and seized control of the Mineo family and their assets. With the assassination, Masseria became the most powerful boss in New York.

Joe Masseria

Nineteen-thirty-one brought about more change for the Masseria family. Joe Masseria had a fight on his hands and his name was Salvatore Maranzano. His family had quietly taken uproots in New York and with his leadership had taken a large chunk of Masseria's business. In April of 1931 seeing the shift in power, some of Masseria's own members murdered Masseria in a restaurant allowing Maranzano to take control of his family. Maranzano declared himself the Capo D tutti Capi (boss of bosses) of all New York. Maranzano was no idiot.

He knew one man would not reign supreme for long, so he divided the New York gangs into "Five Families" and kept the top seat for himself.

Lucky Luciano

In September 1931, just five months after creating the five families, Lucky Luciano called on a small team of assassins to murder Maranzano. Once completed, Lucky and his family (later known as Genovese) further organized the five families creating "The Commission" where each boss of the five families would hold a seat. This Commission would reign as the supreme leader of

New York for generations arbitrating disputes between families and preventing gang warfare.

In the same month, Luciano replaced the acting boss of the D'Aquila/Mineo gang, with mobster Vincent Mangano calling them the Mangano family. Mangano was given a seat on the commission. Mangano led the family with old mob traditions teaching the members honor, tradition, and respect above all else. He also led his family into extortion, horse betting, union racketeering, and murder. He's credited with starting the most feared group of hired killers ever known to the mafia, Murder Incorporated. This group of mainly Jewish Americans was hired by several of the five families to do their dirty work. The most feared of the group was Mangano family underboss Albert Anastasia.

Mangano and his brother Philip didn't mesh well with Anastasia although they worked with each other for several years; they were not close and rarely agreed. Mangano didn't trust Anastasia and as Albert's power within Murder Incorporated grew, so did Mangano's distrust. In April 1951, 20 years after appointment by Luciano as boss of the Mangano crime family, Vincent Mangano was found murdered, and his brother disappeared.

The Commission condemned Anastasia for the murders, and although he denied involvement, they had no choice but to put him in control of the Mangano family. Thus the Anastasia family was born with Albert firmly in control and an up-and-coming member named Carlo Gambino as his second in command. In 1952 with help from Frank Costello boss of the Luciano crime family Anastasia had gained control over the commission.

As a feared gun, Anastasia's control was short lived. He made a series of mistakes in the eyes of the Commission. He ordered the murder of a man who aided in the capture of a notorious bank robber Willie Sutton. He also opened competition casinos in Cuba enraging Meyer Lansky who opened casino's years earlier. It was the final act of disobedience, Anastasia had to go.

In 1957 Genovese and Meyer Lansky called on Anastasia's underboss Carlo Gambino to aid with the take down of Anastasia. With the backing of the Commission, they offered Gambino the top spot in the Anastasia family. In May of the same year Costello escaped a Genovese-organized assassination attempt and quickly resigned as boss. Shortly after, Gambino learned Costello and

Anastasia were working on their own plot to take down Genovese.

In October of 1957 while Anastasia was sitting in the barbershop at Park Sheraton Hotel in Manhattan, several masked assassins entered and fired several rounds into Anastasia killing him instantly. With Anastasia's death, Gambino was promoted by the Commission as boss of the Anastasia family, what is now the Gambino crime family. He appointed Aniello (Neil) Dellacroce in 1965 as underboss.

Over his reign the Gambino crime family gained a strong influence over the construction industry. They influenced the teamsters and unions that controlled the building materials coming into New York. At any given time the Gambino's could bring the entire construction industry to a stop if they chose.

October 15, 1976 Carlo Gambino's 19-year rule ended after he suffered a heart attack and died. As he directed before his death, Paul Castellano an up-and-coming Mafioso and keen business leader took over the Gambino family. Neil Dellacroce remained in the underboss position and was instructed by Castellano to control the traditional

Cosa Nostra activities while he worked the more white- collar activities involving embezzlement and construction schemes.

Paul Castellano

By the early 1980's Castellano created a barrier from the family and him. Dellacroce was the only person allowed to speak with the boss and deliver his messages and actions to the family. Several made members found this alienation to be a slap in the face. One of Castellano's biggest critics was a tough Italian with a large following within the family named John Gotti.

Gotti followed the old school Mafioso traditions closely. He felt the boss of the family needed to show respect to the made members and Castellano

was doing anything but. Gotti admired and
respected Dellacroce who also followed old school
rules. Dellacroce who was in failing health, kept
Gotti and the defectors at ease with Castellano
until Dellacroce's death on December 2, 1985.
Two weeks later, Gotti seized power having
Castellano and his underboss Tommy Bilotti
murdered outside the Sparks Steak House on
December 16, 1985.

John Gotti

Gotti's control over the Gambino crime family
lasted for 7 years. Many of them spent in the court
room as Gotti was tried over and over. He earned
the nickname "Teflon Don" for earning acquittals
in each case. Finally on April 2, 1992 Gotti and his
Consigliere Frank Locascio were convicted and
received life sentences without the possibility of
parole. Gotti continued to rule the family from

prison and left the day-to-day to capo's John D'Amico, and Nicholas Corozzo. Gotti died in prison in 2002. Since Gotti's death, several men have taken control of the family including Gotti's son John "Junior" Gotti.

This is the rise and fall of the Gambino's last Godfather

Gotti's Early Life

John Joseph Gotti, Jr. was born on October 27, 1940, in New York City. He was the fifth child of John J. Gotti, Sr. and his wife, Fannie, who were both Italian immigrants. John was the fifth of 13 children in a family whose only income came from their father's unpredictable work as a day laborer. Due to poor medical care some of his siblings died during childhood. Gotti's father was described in early writings as a hardworking immigrant from the Neapolitan section of Italy.

Young John, left, walks hand-in-hand with his brother, Peter, as their mother, Fannie, looks on.

Years later, Gotti would tell a very different story about his father to Salvatore "Sammy the Bull" Gravano (the Gambino Family underboss who would become the most infamous mob rat in America):

"These fuckin' bums that write books," Gotti complained, *"they're worse than us. My fuckin' father was born in New Jersey. He ain't never been in Italy his whole fuckin' life. My mother neither. The guy never worked a fuckin' day in his life. He was a rolling stone; he never provided for the family. He never did nothin'. He never earned nothin'. And we never had nothin'."*

While this description of his father's work habits was overblown, the family was raised in a dirt-poor, poverty-ridden section of the South Bronx. By the time Gotti was ten; his father had saved enough money to move the family to the Sheepshead Bay neighborhood of Brooklyn. This proved to be a definite step up from their four-room flat in the South Bronx. A year later, another move placed the family in an area of Brooklyn known as East New York.

At an early age, young "Johnny Boy" learned to use his fists. He had a quick temper and a burning anger as he looked on in disdain at those who had a better life. Instead of aspiring to become a businessman or doctor, his goal was to be one of the wiseguys he saw on a daily basis hanging around the Brooklyn street corners. Thus, Gotti had barely turned twelve before he was caught up in the street activity of the local mobsters. Along with two of his brothers Peter and Richard, Gotti became part of a gang that ran errands for an underground club in the neighborhood run by Carmine Fatico. Fatico was a captain in the local Gambino family, the largest of the five organized crime families in New York City. Through his activities with the club, Gotti met Aniello Dellacroce, who became his life-long mentor.

While Gotti was getting a street education, he seldom had time for a formal one. A habitual truant, when he was in school his teachers considered him a disturbing distraction. Because he was a class bully and a routine discipline problem, they showed little concern over his absence.

By 1952 Gotti, was working as a chore boy in an underground club which was run by the head of the local largest organized crime family, Gambino, Carmine Fatico. He met with Aniello Dellacroce there, who became his mentor later.

In 1954, Gotti was injured while participating in a robbery for some local hoods. He and some other kids were in the process of stealing a portable cement mixer from a construction site when the mixer tipped over landing on Gotti's toes, crushing them. After spending most of the summer of his fourteenth year in the hospital, Gotti was back on the street with a new gait that would last him for life.

By the time he was sixteen Gotti quit school for good and became a member of the Fulton-Rockaway Boys, a teenage gang named for an intersection in Brooklyn. Gotti rose rapidly to leadership. The Fulton-Rockaway Boys differed from other "turf-minded" teen gangs in that they were into a higher level of criminality. Gang members stole automobiles, fenced stolen goods and rolled drunks.

Also, with brothers Peter and Richard, Gotti teamed up with two other young men who would become life-long friends. The first was Angelo Ruggiero, a hulking youth whose penchant for non-stop chatter earned him the nickname "Quack-Quack." The second was Wilfred "Willie Boy" Johnson, an amateur boxer whose father was of American Indian descent. Johnson was constantly teased and degraded about his roots, and because of it, he could never become a "made" member of the Mafia because of it.

With the influence of the Gambino family, Gotti became the captain of the 'Fulton-Rockaway' gang. He used to get involved in robberies and car-jackings.

Gotti went to Franklin K. Lane High School where he was considered a bully and constant discipline problem until he dropped out at 16.

Between 1957 and 1961, while a member of the Fulton-Rockaway Boys, Gotti pursued a life of crime on a full-time basis. His arrest record included street fighting, public intoxication, and car theft. By his 21st birthday, Gotti was arrested five times. Each time the charges were dismissed or reduced to a probationary sentence.

By the age of 18, the police department ranked Gotti as a low-level associate in the Fatico crew.

1960's
John Gotti the Family Man

Around 1960, when he was twenty, Gotti met and fell in love with Victoria DiGiorgio. The petite, raven-haired beauty was born to a Jewish father. Her parents divorced when she was still an infant and she later took the last name of her stepfather. Two years younger than Gotti, DiGiorgio dropped out of high school during her senior year. The two were married on March 6, 1962 almost a full year after the birth of their first child, Angela.

The marriage proved to be a stormy one, with many fights and periods of separation. Yet despite their problems, the couple went on to have two more children in rapid succession: a second daughter, Victoria, and John A., who became known as "Junior."

Around this time, Gotti actually tried his hand at legitimate work for the sake of his family: a coat factory presser and a truck driver's assistant. But this was not the life that John wanted. He grew up in the midst of the mafia wise guys and that was where he felt he needed to be.

It wasn't long before John would turn all of his energies back toward a life of crime. Victoria Gotti disparaged her husband's career. She disliked how it made her live. Once, when Gotti was away serving a three-year stretch, she was forced to apply for public welfare.

Pictured from top left are son John, daughter Victoria, his wife, Victoria, Frankie and daughter Angel. A fifth child, Peter, was born in 1974.

Another time she took her husband to court for non-support. Years later FBI bugs would pick up conversations where Gotti talked about his wife, stating, "The woman is driving me crazy!"

Gotti spent his first time in jail, a 20-day period, in 1963 when he was arrested with Salvatore Ruggiero, Angelo's younger brother. They were in an automobile that had been reported stolen from a rental car agency. Gotti's crimes during the early to mid-1960s were mostly petty in nature mostly larceny, unlawful entry, and possession of bookmaking records. In 1966 as well, he would spend several months in jail for an attempted theft.

Yet 1966 proved to be a banner year for the Brooklyn hood. Gotti moved his family to Ozone Park in Queens, New York, the budding criminal quickly became a major player in the Gambino hijacking crew. Gotti became an associate of a Mafia crew headed by Carmine Fatico and his brother Daniel.

Fatico and his crew moved from East New York to a storefront near Gotti's home in Queens. The group's headquarters was disguised as a non-profit organization called the Bergin Hunt and Fish Club, and the Faticos answered to Gambino Family underboss, Aniello Dellacroce. Gotti's criminal career as hijacker began as a member of the Bergin crew. The crew's target, as well as the target of the other New York crime families, was the massive John F. Kennedy International Airport.

While not a great hijacker, Gotti was successful enough to move his family to a nicer apartment in Brooklyn. He and Victoria soon had their fourth child, a second son, whom they named Frank.

On November 27, 1967 Gotti and another crew member – either Angelo Ruggiero or another of Gotti's brothers, Gene – forged the name of a forwarding company agent and then took a rented truck to JFK's United cargo area and drove off with $30,000 worth of merchandise, a good portion of it in women's clothes. Four days later, the FBI was watching as Angelo and Gotti loaded up again with women's clothing, this time at a Northwest Airlines cargo terminal.

Once outside the airport, an automobile containing Gene Gotti pulled alongside. The FBI swooped in and arrested the three men, finding Gotti in the rear of the truck hiding behind several boxes. During the subsequent investigation, United employees identified John Gotti as the man who had signed for the earlier stolen merchandise.

He was arrested for the United hijacking in February 1968. In April, while out on bail, he was arrested a third time for hijacking---this time for stealing a load of cigarettes worth nearly $500,000 outside a restaurant on the New Jersey Turnpike.

At the urging of Carmine Fatico, the Gotti brothers and Angelo hired defense attorney Michael Coiro to represent them. John pled guilty to the Northwest hijacking and was sentenced to four years at the Lewisburg Federal Penitentiary in Pennsylvania.

Prosecutors dropped the charges in the cigarette hijacking, and Coiro was able to get the judge to let Gotti plead guilty in the United theft, while allowing his Lewisburg time to serve as the penalty. Gotti served less than three years of his sentence at Lewisburg, from May 1969 to January 1972.

1970s

After his release from prison, the first order of business for Gotti was to get a legitimate job. John was put on the payroll of Victoria's stepfather's construction company. While Victoria may have wished that her husband would begin a new life, she was resigned to the fact that she could never change him. Shortly after his return she was pregnant with the couple's last child, another son, whom they named Peter. Years later, Victoria would tell a detective inquiring into her husband's activities, "I don't know what he does. All I know is, he provides."

The crew Gotti returned to at the Bergin club consisted mainly of associates. The made members had grown old and a Mafia edict in 1957 had prevented the making of any new ones. Gotti possessed the most moxy of the crewmembers, and when Carmine Fatico was indicted for loansharking and stopped frequenting the club, he used Gotti to oversee the day-to-day activities there.

At the age of 31, Gotti became the acting capo of the Bergin crew while the captain faced loan-sharking charges, with the blessing of Dellacroce.

The Bergin crew under Gotti was young and hungry. Looking to make money, they naturally gravitated toward dealing in narcotics. The unwritten law of the underworld as it pertained to drugs was, "You deal, you die." This had allegedly been decreed at the infamous Apalachin Summit in November 1957, and was carried forward by Carlo Gambino. The more practiced rule was that you could not get caught, and if you did, you faced certain death. A portion of the money from drug deals was always kicked up to the bosses, who chose to look the other way as long as the money rolled in and no one associated with the family ended up in jail.

By May 1972, as Gotti assumed control of the Bergin crew, several members had already become confidential informants for the FBI, or were on their way to it. This group included Willie Boy Johnson and William Battista. Over the years, the government received conflicting reports from these informants as to John Gotti's actual involvement in narcotics. Johnson always maintained that Gotti was not involved and that he toed the line on the no-drug policies of Gambino, and later, of Paul Castellano.

Gotti's first step up the mob ladder came at the expense of Carmine Fatico's legal woes. Gotti's next step would come in a similar manner, but this time it was Dellacroce's problems with the law.

Aniello Dellacroce and John Gotti hit it off right away. In many ways they were like two peas in a pod. In Gotti: Rise and Fall, authors Jerry Capeci and Gene Mustain give this insight into Dellacroce's personality: "...he was Carlo's bad cop. He was fierce, violent, foul-mouthed and clever, and Carlo relied on him when a mix of treachery and trickery was needed to settle some contentious matter." Operating out of the Ravenite Social Club on Mulberry Street in the heart of Manhattan's Little Italy, Dellacroce was highly visible in the neighborhood – so much so that a 1972 Senate committee investigating organized crime actually identified him as the boss of the Gambino Family.

Another thing Dellacroce and Gotti had in common was their bad habit of losing big in gambling. In 1968, Dellacroce was indicted for income tax evasion after reporting an income of

$10,400 when his actual income exceeded $130,000. In addition, the IRS discovered that, while on a three-day vacation in Puerto Rico, Dellacroce had lost more in gambling then he claimed as income for the entire year. Dellacroce was sentenced to a year in prison, and then after he refused to testify before a grand jury, five more were added on, even though he was granted immunity.

With Fatico keeping a low profile and Dellacroce in prison, Gotti, still in the status of an associate, began making regular visits to family boss Carlo Gambino. Years later, Gotti would be overheard on a bug calling Gambino a "rat mother fucker" and a "back door mother fucker" for never promoting him, but in 1973 the young hood stood in awe of "Don Carlo."

A student of Niccolo Machiavelli, the Italian philosopher, Gambino had a habit of quoting from "The Prince." Later while in prison, Gotti would also study the writings of Machiavelli, to the point where he could quote whole parables. Gotti strutted proudly in front of the Bergin crew as he relayed orders from the revered family boss. Although Gambino's edict to stay clear of drug dealing fell on deaf ears, other orders were obeyed.

One of the rulings that came down from Gambino was that family members were to stop the practice of kidnapping other criminals, which at the time was "in vogue." Gambino put the ban in effect after the kidnapping and murder of Manny Gambino, Don Carlo's nephew.

The killing of Manny Gambino, and the subsequent murder of Irish mobster James "Jimmy" McBratney, would become part of the Gotti myth.

The Death of Manny Gambino

In the early 1970s a wave of kidnappings took place in New York City. Incredible as it may seem, the victims were members and associates of the city's crime families. In *Tough Guy: The True Story of "Crazy" Eddie Maloney*, co-authors William Hoffman and Eddie Maloney discuss the kidnappings Eddie and his gang were involved in. Maloney also details his friendship with Jimmy McBratney.

The two men met when both were incarcerated at Greenhaven State Prison in New York. Maloney described McBratney as a devoted family man who stood six-foot-three and weighed 250 pounds. A weight lifter, McBratney could bench-press 400 pounds. Maloney continues: "Jimmy McBratney was locked up for armed robbery. He was quiet, a listener and learner, and soon we were discussing heists we might do together. He knew about guns and wanted to become a collector, but closest to his heart were his wife and two small children and their house on Staten Island, and his goal of saving enough to own a nightclub. I learned Jimmy was very loyal to his wife, and that all the talk in the yard about 'broads' upset him. His wife visited regularly and wrote every day."

In October 1972, Maloney became part of a kidnapping ring with McBratney. It was the brainchild of two wiseguys from the Gambino Crime Family - Flippo and Ronnie Miano. Claiming they only wanted ten percent of the ransoms, Flippo told Maloney that his motive for the kidnappings was revenge. "The guys I'm setting up have fucked me and my people on business deals in the past. It'll give me pleasure to see those greedy fucks suffer," Miano boasted.

The kidnapping gang consisted of Maloney, McBratney; Tommy Genovese, a distant relative of Vito's; Warren "Chief" Schurman, and Richie Chaisson. The first kidnapping was of a Gambino capo called "Frank the Wop." The escapade went off without a hitch and the gang got away with $150,000. Over the next two months, the gang completed three more successful body snatches. However, on December 28, 1972 their luck changed. McBratney outlined a plan to grab a Gambino loanshark named "Junior." Late on this bitter cold afternoon, Maloney stuck a gun in Junior's stomach and ordered him into a car. When

Junior put up a fight, Maloney used a gun to hit him over the head a couple of times before shoving him into the back seat and taking off. Two young witnesses to the crime followed them for a while before they were scared off, but not before they recorded the license number and turned it over to a relative with mob connections.

A friend of Maloney's, in whose apartment they were holding Junior, and through whose mother they had rented the abduction car, spilled his guts to the wiseguys after some hoods showed up at his mother's house asking questions. McBratney was in a panic when he realized the mob had his name, as well as Maloney's and Schurman's. After a relatively small ransom, $21,000, was paid, McBratney arrived at the apartment to pick up Schurman and return the victim. Schurman was supposed to have taped Junior's eyes before covering them with sunglasses, but the slow-witted hood had failed to do it right.

After driving a few blocks McBratney suddenly realized Junior's eyes weren't taped. Enraged, he brought the car to a screeching halt. Junior bolted out of the back seat and ran for his life as McBratney fired several shots at him. Meanwhile, Schurman jumped out of the car and retreated to

Maloney's automobile, which was following them. Schurman was sure McBratney would kill him if he ever saw him again, a fact Maloney confirmed.

Maloney suggested to McBratney that he leave the city. McBratney declined the advice and instead decided to keep a machine gun in his car. Just before Maloney was sent back to prison on a parole violation, he and Schurman were drinking in a bar one night when two guys that he described as "stone killers" came in looking for them. The bar manager, a friend of Maloney's, told the pair he hadn't seen them in a while. While away in prison, Maloney saw a newspaper article about the arrest of McBratney's killers, featuring the pictures of John Gotti and Angelo Ruggiero. He claimed that they were the two "stone killers" who had been looking for him that night in the bar.

In his book, Maloney never mentions the kidnapping and killing of Manny Gambino, the murder that McBratney allegedly paid for with his life.

So what really happened to Manny Gambino? In the book, Brick Agent, former FBI Special Agent Anthony Villano talks in detail about the alleged abduction. Villano was tipped off that Manny

Gambino, the son of Carlo's brother Joseph, had been kidnapped. Villano's attempts to help the family were at first rebuffed. A few days later, an attorney for the family called him and asked the FBI to get involved.

Villano reported that the kidnappers asked for $350,000, but the Gambino family claimed they could only come up with $40,000. The agent figured that either Joe Gambino's side of the family was poor or that having $350,000 in cash on hand might arouse the attention of the IRS.

After receiving new ransom orders, Tommy Gambino, Manny's brother, was told where to drive to and he took off with Villano on the floor in the backseat. The money drop was made before agents tailing Villano could get into position to observe it. However, one of the agents recorded the license number of a van that was seen in the area. The group went back to the Gambino home, only to be disappointed when Manny had not returned by the promised hour. Over the next several months, Villano continued investigating. Through a contact, he found out the following:

"Manny had fallen in love with a show-biz blonde. He wanted to leave his family because the girl

refused to have anything more to do with him unless he gave up his wife and went full-time with her. Manny was advised by his betters in the clan to grow up and forget the blonde. In his circles it was okay to have a mistress but it was bad form to leave your wife, particularly if you were a nephew of Carlo Gambino."

Villano also found out that Manny had a few financial problems, most likely due to maintaining two households. Since he was heavy into loanshark operations, many in the family felt that Manny had too much money on the street. Through a snitch, Villano found out that one of the people who was into Manny for a large sum was gambler Robert Sentner, an ex-associate.

Upon hearing the name, Villano realized the van that was spotted the night the ransom was paid had been rented to a Robert Sentner.

Manny Gambino's car was found at the Newark Airport. Villano reports that before his body was brought to the burial site, rigor mortis had set in. He was found buried in the sitting position in a New Jersey dump, near the Earle Naval Ammunition Depot. Robert Sentner and John Kilcullen were arrested on December 4, 1972, and charged with kidnapping. Sentner later confessed to the murder of Gambino, revealed the names of his other two accomplices, and testified against Kilcullen. On June 1, 1973, he pled guilty to manslaughter and was sentenced to fifteen years in prison.

Despite his detailed account of the incident Villano never mentions Jimmy McBratney's name in the book.

Making His Bones

In all likelihood, Jimmy McBratney was identified as a member of the team that abducted Junior, and murdered because of his involvement. McBratney was obviously not an innocent, law-abiding citizen. He had committed armed robbery, kidnapping, and possession of illegal weapons, and – if his aim had been better – may have wounded or killed the Staten Island loan shark. However, it is certain that McBratney did not kidnap and murder Carlo Gambino's nephew, thus showing to be false the fabled notion that Gotti had taken vengeance on him for killing the nephew of the highly respected mob boss. This event, like so many others involving John Gotti, has been twisted to enhance the romanticized image of this popular mob icon, and to boost his popularity.

On the night of May 22, 1973 McBratney was sitting in Snoope's Bar & Grill on Staten Island. Around 11:00 John Gotti, Angelo Ruggiero and Ralph "Ralphie Wigs" Galione entered and surrounded McBratney. They tried to convince him that they were police detectives. The plan was to take him to the parking lot and kill him outside the sight of witnesses. Despite the fact that Galione aimed a gun at him and Ruggiero was holding a pair of handcuffs, McBratney wasn't buying the ruse. "Let's see a badge," he demanded.

With that, Galione fired a round into the ceiling. Bar patrons, who hadn't already run outside or into the cellar, were ordered to stand against the wall. It was now prison muscle against prison muscle, and although McBratney was stronger, he was up against two men, Gotti and Ruggiero. McBratney dragged the two thugs down past the end of the bar before Galione shot him three times at close range, killing him instantly.

In July, Ruggiero and Galione were identified from a police photo-spread by a barmaid and a customer from Snoopes, and the men were then apprehended. However, Gotti had not been identified. A month later, he was overheard by Willie Boy Johnson bragging about the killing. Johnson passed the information along to his FBI handlers. The FBI reported their information to the New York Police Department, which quickly dispatched a detective with Gotti's mug shot to show the witnesses. On October 17, Gotti was indicted by a grand jury for murder.

Gotti, who had been strutting around in the wake of the murder, immediately went into hiding. A little over a year after the McBratney killing, on June 3, 1974, he was finally arrested by FBI agents inside a Brooklyn bar and handed over to the New York Police Department. The information as to his whereabouts had been supplied by Johnson, who was secretly paid $600 for his betrayal.

John Gotti's in-laws were instrumental in putting up the collateral for his release on a $150,000 bail. Victoria's family, which had already provided John with a visible means of support, also purchased a home for the couple in Howard Beach. Once out, Gotti went right back to the Bergin to attend to the overseeing of the crew and his new holdings, which included a restaurant and motel. Gotti was also reported at the time to be the hidden owner of a Queens' disco.

On December 21, 1973, before Ruggiero and Galione could be tried for the McBratney killing, "Ralphie Wigs" was murdered in Brooklyn. When the state brought its case against Ruggiero the defense produced a host of witnesses who swore that Angelo was in New Jersey the night of the murder. The trial ended in a hung jury. Gotti hired Roy M. Cohn as his defense lawyer. A well-known attorney, Cohn handled many high-profile clients in New York, including Dellacroce.

Gotti and Ruggiero were to be tried together in a second trial. Knowing that the earlier trial ended in a hung jury, Cohn surmised correctly that the prosecution might be willing to deal – and Cohn cut a great one. Gotti and Ruggiero pled guilty to attempted manslaughter.

On August 8, 1975, Gotti was sentenced to four years in prison and sent to the Green Haven Correctional Facility located 80 miles north of Queens. Joining Gotti there was Willie Boy Johnson, who, despite his FBI informant status, had been sent away on an armed robbery conviction. Gotti passed the time at Green Haven playing cards, lifting weights and attending courses on Italian culture.

He was released from prison on July 28, 1977, having served less than two years for the murder of McBratney. It was ironic, since he'd once served three years for hijacking women's clothing. To celebrate his return the Bergin crew purchased a brand new Lincoln Mark IV for him. He soon found out that, while he was away, there had been a change in the leadership of the Gambino Family.

Changes at the Top

On October 15, 1976, the grandfatherly-looking Carlo Gambino died of natural causes. Before his death, he let family *consigliere*, Joseph N. Gallo, and key capos, James "Jimmy Brown" Failla and Ettore Zappi, know that he wanted the leadership of the family to pass to his cousin, Paul Castellano.

Yet there was one sticking point to this change: Aniello Dellacroce, the current underboss. On Thanksgiving Day in 1976, Dellacroce was released from prison. Many Gambino Family members believed Dellacroce should have been named boss. His years of loyalty to the family, and the respect and admiration that the street soldiers had for him, were just a few of the reasons.

In December, the upper echelon of the Gambino Family met at the home of capo Anthony "Nino" Gaggi to officially name a new boss. It was a tense situation. Not knowing what might transpire, Gaggi taped a gun under the kitchen table prior to the meeting. He then armed his nephew, Vietnam veteran Dominick Montiglio, with an automatic weapon. Montiglio took up a position in an upstairs apartment, which overlooked a doorway leading out to the driveway of Gaggi's house.

"If you hear any shots from the kitchen," Gaggi instructed Montiglio, "shoot whoever runs out the door."

But there was no shootout. Castellano agreed to keep Dellacroce as family underboss. In accepting Castellano's leadership proposal, Dellacroce was given several crews to oversee, including the Bergin crew of Carmine Fatico.

Then Gotti came home. According to the terms of his parole, he had to have a legitimate job, so in the summer of 1977, he became a salesman for Arc Plumbing & Heating Corporation. Years later, when the president of the plumbing concern was asked at a hearing what function Gotti performed, he replied, "What John does is point out locations."

Gotti set his sights on climbing into Carmine Fatico's position as head of the Bergin crew. Fatico had recently beaten two loansharking cases, but he and his brother Daniel, along with crewmembers Charles and John Carneglia, had been convicted of hijacking. The Faticos pled guilty, hoping to receive probation. One of the government informants reported that Gotti was hoping that his former mentor would be sent away, enabling him to move ahead.

Carmine Fatico received five years' probation, but his reign as capo of the Bergin crew was over, because the terms required that he not associate with known criminals. Occasionally Gotti was to seek the elder Mafioso's counsel, but they would never meet at the Bergin.

Gotti was still considered an associate and could not officially become the "acting capo" of the crew until he became a made member of the Gambino Family. Sometime during the first half of 1977, Angelo Ruggiero (paroled earlier than John) and Gene Gotti (who acted as crew boss in his brother's absence), were both made.

According to an informant, another induction ceremony was planned for later that year upon John's release from the Green Haven Correctional Facility. In this second rite, Gotti and eight other men took the Mafia oath of omerta.

Mafia initiation ritual

To become a full member of the Mafia or Cosa Nostra – to become a "man of honour" – an aspiring member has to pass what some have called, "a Mafia initiation ritual." The ceremony involves significant ritual, oaths, blood, and an agreement is made to follow the rules of the Mafia as presented to the inductee. The first known account of the ceremony dates back to 1877 in Sicily.

The typical sequence of the ceremony according to several distinct descriptions has common features. First, the new recruit is led into the presence of other members and presented by a member; the association is explained including its basic rules; then his finger is pricked with a needle by the officiating member; a few drops of blood are spilled on a card bearing the likeness of a saint; the card is set on fire; finally, while the card is passed rapidly from hand to hand to avoid burns, the novice takes an oath of loyalty to the Mafia family.

The first known account of the ceremony dates back to 1877 in Monreale in an article in the *Giornale di Sicilia* in an account about the

Stuppagghiari, an early Mafia-type organisation. Other early accounts were during a trial against the *Fratellanza* (Brotherhood) in Agrigento (1884) and the *Fratuzzi* (Little Brothers) in Bagheria (1889).

One of the first life accounts of an initiation ceremony was given by Bernardino Verro, a leader of the Fasci Siciliani, a popular social movement of democratic and socialist inspiration, which arose in Sicily in the early 1890s. In order to give the movement teeth and to protect himself from harm, Verro became a member of the *Fratuzzi* in Corleone. In a memoir written many years later, he describes the initiation ritual he underwent in the spring of 1893:

"I was invited to take part in a secret meeting of the Fratuzzi. I entered a mysterious room where there were many men armed with guns sitting around a table. In the center of the table there was a skull drawn on a piece of paper and a knife. In order to be admitted to the *Fratuzzi*, I had to undergo an initiation consisting of some trials of loyalty and the pricking of the lower lip with the tip of the knife: the blood from the wound soaked the skull."

Soon after Verro broke with the Mafia and – according to police reports – became their most bitter enemy. He was killed by the Mafia in 1915 when he was the mayor of Corleone.

The first known account of the ritual in the United States was provided in 1963 by Joe Valachi, who was initiated in 1930, in his testimony for the McClellan Committee, officially known as the Permanent Subcommittee on Investigations of the Committee on Government Operation of the senate in the United States.

Valachi's was a high-profile case, and helped convince the country of the existence of the organization in the United States called the Cosa Nostra, also known as the Mafia. He provided the FBI with first-hand information about the inside of the Mafia, including one of the first ever descriptions of the induction ceremony.

The Mafia solicits select and specific people for membership—one cannot just choose to join up. In Tommaso Buscetta's testimony for the "pizza connection" narcotics trial, he was asked what he did to get into the Cosa Nostra. He answered, "I didn't make out any application to become a member—I was called, I was invited." The way the structure works, an inside member suggests a name, and before the person is seriously considered, they are watched closely for an extended period of time—generally a number of years. The member who put forth the name and those who choose to support the potential member are "held responsible" for everything the new member does and can be killed as a result of a bad choice.

The mafia looks for people that are faithful and someone who will bring money to the organization. The chance to be chosen is highly coveted within that niche..."

Joe Valachi had an extended courtship before he finally consented to join. He was eventually swayed by the argument of Mafiosi Bobby Doyle, who said that a solo career of crime was much more dangerous. Doyle said to Valachi, *"Join us and you will be made. You will earn money and you are not to steal anymore."*

Things had been getting difficult for Valachi in terms of frequent arrests and other consequences of his lifestyle, and he acknowledged the logic of Doyle's argument.

The ceremony is a dinner or a meeting. Several people may be inducted at once. When inducted, "they are 'made' or 'baptized' or 'get their badges'". Other terms used are becoming "wiseguys", "friends", "good fellows", "one of us" or "straightened out".

Valachi gave the most well-known description of the ceremony:

"I sit down at the table. There is wine. Someone put a gun and a knife in front of me. The gun was a .38 and the knife was what we call a dagger. Maranzano [the boss] motions us up and we say some words in Italian. Then Joe Bonanno pricks my finger with a pin and squeezes until the blood comes out. What then happens, Mr. Maranzano says, 'This blood means that we are now one Family. You live by the gun and the knife and you die by the gun and the knife.'"

Valachi was inducted with three others. There were about 40 members present, so the new initiates could "meet the family."

During the Patriarca crime family's induction of 1989 that was taped by the FBI, several other details were discovered. Before the inductee Tortora took the oath, he was told that he would be baptized. *"You were baptized when you were a baby, your parents did it. But now, this time, we gonna baptize you."*

The baptism seems to represent the new stage of life that is beginning. This is one example of the family mentality of the mafia. It is implied that the Mafia is taking the place of the member's family, of his parents.

Further evidence of this mentality can be seen when Tortora is asked if he would kill his brother for the Mafia. This mentality most likely comes about because members are giving their entire lives to the organization. The oaths themselves talk about the family bond, and we can conjecture that the rules of secrecy represent the family loyalty as well as a sense of self-preservation. Despite rivalries, all of the mafia families are seen to be related. Even between groups in Sicily and New York City, there is a sense of brotherhood.

Another variation from Valachi's description found in the 1989 induction recording is when inductee Flamaro specifically had his trigger finger pricked which affirms that there is definite symbolism in the gesture. After this, a compare/buddy was chosen for him, and, unlike other ceremonies described, no mention was made of burning a picture of a saint. In Buscetta's testimony, he said that when his finger was pricked, the blood was transferred to a picture of a saint, which was then burned. Buscetta then swore that if he disobeyed the rules, "my flesh would burn like this saint." A variation on this oath is "As burns this saint, so will burn my soul. I enter alive and I will have to get out dead." Jimmy Fratianno, inducted in 1947, described the Capo pricking his finger and saying, "This drop of blood symbolizes your birth into our family, we are one until death." The ceremony is finished with a kiss administered to both cheeks of the new Mafiosi.

In the past, it was said that to complete the induction process, the potential member was kill someone, though the practice seems to have died out for the most part.

The Mafia Code is remarkably similar to that of not only other crime organizations and societies, but also to that present in American Prisons. Donald Cressey notes that it is basically the same as the thieves' code, which he outlines as having five basic parts:

1. Be loyal to members of the organization. Do not interfere with each other's interest. Do not be an informer.

2. Be rational. Be a member of the team. Don't engage in battle if you can't win....The directive extends to personal life.

3. Be a man of honor. Respect womanhood and your elders. Don't rock the boat....

4. Be a stand-up guy. Keep your eyes and ears open and your mouth shut. Don't sell out....The 'stand-up guy' shows courage and 'heart.' He does not whine or complain in the face of adversity, including punishment, because 'If you can't pay, don't play.'

5. Have class. Be independent. Know your way around the world."

The members were also instructed at the Patriarca ceremony to not let this whole thing inflate their egos and change them. The mafia wanted them for who they were when they were chosen; humility is implied.

Now a made member of the Gambino Family, Gotti's hijacking career officially came to an end. He avoided what were considered "riskier crimes" and settled instead on mob staples, such as gambling and loan sharking. Since Gotti was still on probation, he ordered Bergin crewmembers "not to bring heat on the club." They were told to "stop loitering in front of the Bergin and to park their cars elsewhere." This was a far cry from what his attitude would be years later.

During the late 1970s and early 1980s, the FBI's snitches reported that Gotti lost heavily at gambling and crewmembers were growing concerned because they were unable to make money. It was not unusual for Gotti to drop $30,000 in one night. In February 1981 Gotti opened a gambling den on the second floor of the Bergin club for "family" men only. The game operated every night except Saturday, closing down around 4:00 am.

In early March, the game moved to Manhattan, to a location on Mott Street around the corner from Dellacroce's Ravenite Social Club. The game was very popular and drew many gamblers from throughout the city. The crew finally made money even though Gotti continued to lose heavily. Since he was overseeing the game Gotti could borrow money from the house. In a move typical of him, he became concerned about those who borrowed from the house and ordered an accounting, only to discover that he owed the most – some $55,000. Bugs and taps on the telephone of a crewmember revealed the contempt in which others held Gotti, including Angelo Ruggiero and John's own brother Gene.

One night, a Queens detective squad watched as Wilfred Johnson handed a package to a drug dealer in exchange for a paper bag that he threw into the trunk of his car. Detectives followed Johnson to his home in Brooklyn. When Willie Boy opened the trunk to get the bag, the detectives approached him. The bag contained $50,000, which Johnson quickly claimed came from the gambling operation. Still on probation after having served less than four years of a ten-year sentence, Johnson got scared. He told the officers to take the money, because if his parole officer found out about it he would go back to prison.

Johnson, who was already working as a confidential informant for the FBI, now agreed to do the same for the New York City Police Department. In June 1981, he ratted out the Mott Street gambling club and approximately thirty men were arrested. After spending the night in the Manhattan Criminal Court, the men---represented by attorney Michael Coiro---pled guilty to misdemeanor gambling charges, and were fined $500 and released. The following night, a new operation opened across the street from the raided location. However, the game never regained its former popularity.

1980's

The Tragedy of Frank Gotti

Frank Gotti was the fourth child of John and Victoria Gotti, their second son. Frank Gotti led the life of an average twelve-year-old. He was a good student and enjoyed sports. On March 18, 1980, he borrowed a friend's motorized mini-bike and took a ride around his Howard Beach neighborhood. At the same time, John Favara, a service department manager for a furniture manufacturer, was on his way home from work. Favara was a neighbor of the Gottis.

His house on 86th Street was directly behind the Gotti home on 85th Street. Favara's adopted son, Scott, was a friend of Gotti's son, John, and had enjoyed sleepovers in the Gotti home.

With the sun going down in the late afternoon, young Frank Gotti and the 51 year-old Favara were about to have the proverbial "appointment with destiny." In *Mobstar*, by Jerry Capeci and Gene Mustain, the authors describe what happened next:

"On 157th Avenue, near 87th, a house was under renovation. A dumpster had been placed in the street to collect the debris. It was on Favara's right. Favara did not notice the boy on the mini-bike dash into the street from the other side of the dumpster, and his car struck and killed Frank Gotti."

The death of her son was a crushing blow to Victoria Gotti. She lived for her children. Frank Gotti's funeral was heavily attended by friends. Favara was advised by a local priest not to make an appearance. FBI agents, who normally held surveillance at wakes and funerals, stayed away out of respect for the death of a child.

Two days after the accident, a woman called the 106th Precinct house and said, "The driver of the car that killed Frank Gotti will be eliminated." That same day, Favara received a death threat in the mail.

On March 23, a detective visited the Favara home to warn him about the phone threat. Favara told the detective, "That kind of stuff only happens in the movies."

Naïve to the danger he was in, Favara could not understand why the Gotti family didn't realize the child's death was a tragic accident. A woman's phone call to the Favara home on March 24 spelled out another death threat.

On April 13, Favara's car, which had not been repaired, was stolen. It was recovered less than a mile from his home on May 1.

Nineteen days later, a funeral card from the services for Frank Gotti was left in Favara's mailbox. The following day a picture of Frank Gotti was placed in the mailbox. The next day, May 22, the word "Murderer" was spray-painted on the Favara car.

Favara had been a childhood friend of Anthony Zappi, whose father, Ettore, had been a capo in the Gambino Family. Favara went to Anthony Zappi for advice. Zappi told Favara to move out of the neighborhood and get rid of his automobile, because Victoria became enraged every time she saw it.

While contemplating his decision, he was helped along by Victoria, who attacked him on May 28th with an aluminum baseball bat. Favara was treated at a local hospital, but refused to file charges. Favara took Zappi's advice and put his home up for sale. On July 28, three days before he was to close on the sale of his house, Favara was abducted while leaving work. Several people watched as Favara was clubbed over the head and thrown into a van.

He and his car were never seen again. A diner owner who witnessed the attack and described it to police soon received a visit from three hulking hoods who sat silently for fifteen minutes staring at him. The diner owner avoided the police, sold his business and moved away.

John and Victoria had conveniently been in Fort Lauderdale, Florida, when the abduction took place. The FBI canvassed their informants for information. William Battista reported that while "Gotti did not initially want revenge," an alleged eyewitness had claimed that Favara had been speeding and had run a stop sign just prior to hitting Frank.

Battista claimed that since Victoria had been "so distraught" over the death of her son, John promised her revenge. When the couple returned from the south, detectives questioned them. About Favara, Victoria claimed, *"I don't know what happened to him. I am not sorry if something did. He never sent me a [sympathy] card. He never apologized. He never even got his car fixed."* John's response was similar, if not rehearsed. *"I don't know what happened. I am not sorry if something did happen. He killed my kid."*

Frank Gotti would have turned 13 on October 18, 1980. Victoria took the opportunity to place two "In Memoriam" notices, one from her children and a second from her and John, in the New York Daily News. Every year since, on the anniversary of Frank's death, the notices appear. As the children began their own families, the number of notices grew. Each of Frank Gotti's siblings named a son in his memory.

On March 8, 2001, Jerry Capeci's "This Week in Gang Land," ran an exclusive account of the John Favara disappearance. In the article, Capeci states that the story was put together from information from present and former law enforcement people who were connected with the case. Capeci identifies eight crewmembers – Angelo Ruggiero, Willie Boy Johnson, Gene Gotti, John and Charles Carneglia, Anthony Rampino, Richard Gomes and Iggy Alogna – as having played a role in the abduction and slaying.

It played out like this: as Favara approached his automobile he spotted the men and turned to run. John Carneglia dropped him with two shots from a .22 caliber, silencer-equipped pistol. Favara gasped, "No. No. Please, my wife," as he struggled to get off the ground. Gomes, a former hood from Providence, Rhode Island, who had joined the Gotti crew in the late 1970s, cracked Favara over the head with a two-by-four, picked him up and threw him in a van. Another crewmember took the victim's keys and followed in Favara's car.

One account says that while alive he was dismembered with a chainsaw and stuffed into a barrel filled with concrete and dumped in the ocean or buried on the chop shop lot somewhere.

While Charles Carneglia disposed of the barrel in the ocean off Brooklyn, his brother John crushed Favara's car at the salvage yard. No one was ever arrested for the abduction and murder. Favara's wife and two sons moved out of Howard Beach, having John declared legally dead in 1983.

In November 2004, informants led the FBI to excavate a parking lot in New York City suspected to be a mob graveyard and the site of Favara's body. While two bodies were found, Favara's was not.

Previously prosecutors believed Favara's remains were stuffed in a barrel of concrete and tossed off a Sheepshead Bay pier, but Brooklyn federal court papers filed by federal prosecutors the week of January 5, 2009, contain allegations that Carneglia killed Favara and disposed of his body in acid.

Mob Politics

John Gotti was building the inner circle of his Bergin crew into a powerful outfit. Those closest to Gotti were Angelo Ruggiero, who was looked upon as the number two man; brother Gene, who at times could be just as brutal as his older brother; John Carneglia, who ran the auto-salvage business; Anthony "Tony Roach" Rampino, whose physical features led to his nickname; and Willie Boy Johnson.

Rampino and Johnson served as Gotti's chief loan collectors. Gotti also employed his other brothers, Peter and Richard. Peter took care of the Bergin club, while Richard was assigned the Our Friends Social Club, located around the corner from the Bergin. Gotti insisted that all his men put in regular appearances at the Bergin and got irritated if anyone failed to check in within 48 hours.

During this period, from the late 1970s into the early 1980s, the FBI was building a crew of their own - a crew of informants. In addition to the aforementioned Willie Boy Johnson and William Battista, the bureau had also turned Salvatore "Crazy Sal" Polisi, Matthew Traynor and Anthony

Cardinale, a heavy drug user whom Angelo Ruggiero had met in Attica.

Despite carrying on crimes, this quartet of murderers was constantly feeding new information about Gotti's activities to their FBI handlers. Gotti, on the other hand, was not blind to the efforts of law enforcement and knew that several of the telephones the gang used were tapped.

Cautious with the information he shared with crewmembers over the bugged lines, he never hesitated when it came to placing his bets. In addition to the telephone taps and informants, listening devices ("bugs") had been installed in the Bergin club, which were picking up a variety of conversations from the hoodlums that congregated there.

After the death of his son, John Gotti's gambling habits became more reckless. This was an observation that William Battista passed along to the FBI. The government informant was not alone in his opinion. Paul Castellano, the boss of the family, voiced his own concerns to Dellacroce. Although Dellacroce passed it off as Gotti's way of dealing with grief, Castellano was still unhappy.

Jerry Capeci and Gene Mustain discuss Castellano's position in *Gotti: Rise and Fall*:

"Still, Gotti's gambling made Paul question his fitness for leadership. With typical Sicilian bias for people of Neapolitan origin, Paul already had a low opinion of Gotti's fitness. Like his ancestors, he thought Neapolitans were brash, garish, unreliable, too emotional."

Both Gotti and Dellacroce questioned Castellano's leadership skills. Castellano, who was never considered a "street" person, didn't understand Gotti or the men who made up his crew – and never took the time to try. Castellano retreated to his palatial home on Todt Hill on Staten Island, where he preferred to deal with a few chosen family members. During the early half of the 1980s, the relationship between Castellano and the Dellacroce/Gotti crew would continue to deteriorate steadily.

Drugs and the Ruggiero Phone Tap

As information was obtained from the FBI's confidential informants, a picture of the drug dealing going on by the Bergin crew began to unfold. Yet it was never clear how big a role John Gotti played in the crew's drug involvement. Outwardly he was still pushing the family line of no drugs, but there is little doubt that he prospered from the enormous profits crewmembers earned.

By the early 1980s, the government was beginning to investigate New York's five organized crime families. FBI Special Agent Bruce Mouw was selected to head what was called the "Gambino squad." The determined agent worked to develop confidential informants inside the family and managed to identify the hierarchy of the Gambino Crime Family.

Starting with information supplied by "Source Wahoo" (the secret FBI code name assigned to Willie Boy Johnson) that Angelo Ruggiero's home telephone was safe; the FBI proceeded to "launch an electronic assault" against the mobster known as "Quack Quack." On November 9, 1981, a tap was placed on the home phone of Ruggiero. One of the reasons Ruggiero was chosen was because his brother, Salvatore, had become a millionaire from dealing drugs on his own and was currently a fugitive from justice.

One day after Angelo talked to Gene Gotti, using the word "babania" (a street name for heroin); the Gambino Squad approached a judge for a warrant for further electronic surveillance. During the early part of 1982, Ruggiero had moved from Howard Beach to Cedarhurst, Long Island.

Agents disguised as construction workers, with information again supplied by Willie Boy Johnson, planted listening devices in Ruggiero's kitchen, dining room and basement den, and tapped the Princess phone in his daughter's bedroom. In addition, they increased physical surveillance, even allowing Angelo to spot them in hopes that this would instigate more discussion from him.

On May 6, 1982, Salvatore Ruggiero chartered a private plane at an airport in New Jersey to fly him and his wife to southern Florida to look at some investment property. Salvatore, a fugitive from the government for six years, had been hiding out in Florida, Ohio and Pennsylvania. The plane crashed into the Atlantic Ocean off the coast of southern Georgia, killing everyone on board.

Salvatore's death set off a chain of events that would result in an internecine war in the Gambino Family and propel John Gotti into leadership. After being notified of the fatal accident, Angelo, Gene Gotti and John Carneglia quickly descended on Salvatore's New Jersey hideout to remove paperwork, valuables and all the heroin they could find.

Attorney Michael Coiro, who had represented Angelo in the past, arrived from Florida two days after Salvatore's death to help Angelo resolve legal issues involving his brother's estate. While the two were meeting at Angelo's home, Gambino Family capo Frank DeCicco arrived to offer his condolences. As agents listened in, Coiro told DeCicco, "Gene found the heroin."

Several weeks after the memorial service for Salvatore, Coiro was still around helping Angelo. During a bugged conversation at Angelo's home, the FBI picked up the following exchange between Angelo, Coiro and Gene Gotti as Ruggiero talked about unloading the heroin:

Ruggiero: *If I get some money, will you hold it?*

Coiro: *Yeah.*

Gene: *Nobody is to know but us. You're not our lawyer, you're one of us as far as I'm concerned.*

Coiro: *I know it, Gene, I feel that way too.*

As the months dragged on, so did the tape recorders picking up all the incriminating evidence pouring out of the mouths of Angelo Ruggiero and the visitors to his home.

During this period the heroin was sold, to which Ruggiero was heard exclaiming, "There's a lot of profit in heroin." With those profits Gene Gotti and John Carneglia flew to Florida and made a heroin purchase from one of Salvatore's former suppliers.

Bruce Mouw held off making any arrests in hopes that he could catch John Gotti at Ruggiero's home or on one of the phone taps discussing the heroin. It didn't happen. It was claimed that Gotti felt that as acting capo he should never visit the home of a "soldier."

On August 8, 1983, seventeen months after Salvatore Ruggiero's death, the Gambino Squad arrested Angelo, Gene Gotti, John Carneglia, Michael Coiro, and Mark Reiter. In addition to the heroin discussions caught on mountains of tapes, the bugs and phone taps picked up Ruggiero making a plethora of disparaging remarks about Paul Castellano. The battle Castellano waged to get these tapes would eventually lead to his demise.

Problems for 'Big Paulie'

Nearly six years would pass before a conviction would occur as a result of the indictments issued against Angelo Ruggiero, Gene Gotti and the others. By that time Paul Castellano was long gone and John Gotti had become the "Teflon Don."

Castellano's problems had begun to mount in the early 1980s, as the government set their sights on the mob bosses of New York City's five organized crime families. With the recent drug indictments of members of Gotti's crew, Castellano felt he needed to act. To calm the situation, Ruggiero convinced Aniello Dellacroce to approach the irritated boss with a contrived story that they were only sorting out Angelo's brother's affairs. Salvatore was neither a member nor an associate of the Gambino Family, and, not being a subordinate to Castellano, could not be held accountable for disobeying any family rules. This plan would hold Castellano at bay until the actual FBI tapes could be handed over to defense attorneys.

Castellano did not realize that the information Ruggiero spread across the telephone lines, recorded by FBI phone taps, provided the government with enough probable cause to enter and bug his palatial estate. By early 1984, the Gambino Family boss was facing an indictment as the result of an investigation into another crew, that of former capo Roy "the Killing Machine" DeMeo. Despite the fact that Castellano had DeMeo killed, when the indictment was issued, the boss and DeMeo crewmembers were facing charges of "murder for hire, drug dealing, an international car-theft operation, child pornography, and prostitution."

In addition, Castellano's attorneys informed him he was also facing indictment in two other RICO cases. The first was referred to as the "hierarchy" case, which would eventually result in the convictions of Gambino Family underboss Joseph "Piney" Armone and one-time consigliere Joseph N. Gallo. The second case was known as the "Commission" case, for which Castellano would be indicted.

It wasn't just Castellano who was under siege in the spring of 1985, it was the entire Gambino Crime Family. In addition to the "hierarchy" case, indictments were issued against John and Gene Gotti, Neil Dellacroce and his son Armond, John Carneglia, Willie Boy Johnson, Anthony "Tony

Roach" Rampino, and several others. Using the RICO statute, the mobsters were indicted for crimes ranging from murder to loansharking. The indictments were the culmination of several years of work by assistant United States attorney Diane Giacalone, who represented the Eastern District of New York. Described in Mob Star as "outspoken, strong-willed and occasionally tempestuous," the 31 year-old former tax attorney had grown up in the Ozone Park neighborhood, and while attending school, had passed by the Bergin Hunt and Fish Club daily.

One of the things Giacalone discovered was that Willie Boy Johnson was a confidential FBI informant. She quickly tried to convince Johnson to become a government witness and to testify against his long-time friend John Gotti and his Bergin crewmates. Johnson was in fear for his life, as well as the safety of his family. "I'll be killed," he told the prosecutor. "My family will be slaughtered." Gotti was soon made aware of Johnson's treachery. In *Gotti: Rise and Fall*, Capeci and Mustain reveal his reaction:

"'I'm gonna give you a pass, and I give you my word no one will bother you," Gotti told Willie Boy. "After we win this case, you won't be able to

be in the life again. But you'll get a job, you'll have your family, and you'll be all right.'"

Despite Johnson's plea to be granted bail with the others, Giacalone convinced the judge to keep Willie Boy in protective custody, where he would remain for over a year before the case came to trial. Meanwhile, government informant William Battista found out that Giacalone was looking to bring him into the case. Battista responded by grabbing his wife and fleeing the area, and they have not been seen since.

In the spring of 1985, Paul Castellano turned 70. He would not see 71. Still demanding to hear the Ruggiero tapes, the aging leader backed off again when it was revealed that Neil Dellacroce was dying of cancer. Castellano figured that when Dellacroce died, he could press for the tapes without incurring the wrath of his underboss. When Castellano finally got to hear the tapes during the late summer of 1985, he formulated a plan of action, but still held off while Dellacroce remained alive.

Thinking that Castellano would have them killed Gotti and Ruggiero began plotting "Big Paulie's" demise. They first lined up support in their own family from Gravano, DeCicco, Armone and Robert DiBernardo---an independent operator without his own crew, who was a good earner for the family. The conspirators then "reached out" to the Bonanno, Colombo and Lucchese Families. The Genovese Family led by long-time Castellano ally Vincent "the Chin" Gigante, was not included in the Gambino Family's restructuring plan.

When Neil Dellacroce died on December 2, 1985, Castellano refused to go to the wake, claiming he wanted to avoid government surveillance.

This breach of mob family etiquette only strengthened resistance against him. And Gotti saw the behavior as disrespectful and, according to later testimony, he decided to take action.

Castellano then named his driver/body guard, Thomas Bilotti, to the position of underboss. Castellano announced he was going to close Dellacroce's Ravenite social club and reassign the old Fatico Bergin members to other crews.

Castellano's reorganization plans would meet a swift and deadly response. Two weeks later, on December 16, 1985, Castellano was gunned down outside of Sparks Steak House in Manhattan. Gotti was made boss soon after.

Sparks Steak House

Sparks Steak House

On the late, cold afternoon of December 16, 1985, unsuspecting New Yorkers, hustling home from a long day's work, were about to witness a public underworld execution. In *Underboss*, Sammy Gravano and Peter Maas describe the setup:

'The more we thought about it, the better it looked,' Sammy said. 'We concluded that nine days before Christmas, around five to six o'clock at night, in the middle of

Manhattan, in the middle of rush hour, in the middle of the crush of all them shoppers buying presents, there would be literally thousands of people on the street, hurrying this way and that. The hit would only take a few seconds, and the confusion would be in our favor. Nobody would be expecting anything like this, least of all Paul. And being able to disappear afterwards in the crowds would be in our favor. So we decide this is when and where it's going to happen.'

The day before the assassinations of Paul Castellano and Thomas Bilotti were to take place, eleven conspirators met at Gravano's office on Stillwell Avenue. According to Gravano, the four designated shooters were Vincent Artuso, John Carneglia, Eddie Lino and his brother-in-law Salvatore Scala. The designated back-up shooter, Anthony "Tony Roach" Rampino, would be standing across the street from Sparks Steak House, while Angelo Ruggiero, Joseph Watts and Iggy Alogna would be stationed at 46th Street and Second Avenue to facilitate the escape. Frank DeCicco would be inside the restaurant where a meeting was to take place. He would be joined there by capos James Failla and Daniel Marino, who were not part of the plot.

A December 16, 1999 article in Jerry Capeci's "This Week in Gang Land" claims Gravano mistakenly named Alogna as a member of the hit team. Stating "informed sources" say Dominick Pizzonia was the other man present. There is also another version as to who was present inside Sparks Steak House. According to Remo Franceschini in his book *A Matter of Honor*, the retired police lieutenant claims:

On December 16 Big Paul had arranged to meet Neil Dellacroce's son Buddy Dellacroce at Sparks Steak House on East 46th Street. Frank DeCicco set it up. Castellano was going to pay homage, to explain why he hadn't come to the wake and offered condolences, to make amends and praise the dead.

It wouldn't be until the afternoon of the planned murders that the actual hit team knew who their targets were. Huddled in a park on Manhattan's Lower East Side, the group went over the final details of the murder plot.

The four shooters were dressed alike - long light colored trench coats and black fur Russian, or Cossack, style hats. The reasoning for this was to draw attention to the outfits, not the men wearing them.

Gravano told the FBI that he and Gotti arrived near Sparks Steak House close to five o'clock in a Lincoln driven by John. Famed New York Police Detective Joseph Coffey, in an interview with Court TV's Rikki Klieman years later, doubted the two were in the vicinity of the restaurant.

Gravano claimed that after circling the block, they parked where from their vantage point they would have a clear view of the front of the restaurant. Moments later Bilotti in a black Lincoln pulled alongside Gotti's car and waited for the light to change. Using a walkie-talkie Gravano notified the others that Castellano was proceeding through the intersection.

Bilotti steered the Lincoln into an open space in front of Sparks and got out. As Castellano alighted from the vehicle, the hit men moved in. "Big Paulie" was hit six times in the head and killed instantly. When the shooting began, the unarmed Bilotti stooped to look through the driver's side window only to see his boss's execution, unaware that killers were now aiming at him. As the shooters assigned to Bilotti opened fire, Artuso's gun jammed. However, the gunfire from the second assassin dropped the newly crowned underboss and Carneglia, who had finished blasting away at Castellano, rounded the automobile and put the finishing touches on Bilotti.

The assassination squad ran past scrambling pedestrians, who were running for cover, and made their way to Second Avenue and the getaway cars. Gotti and Gravano calmly drove past Sparks. As he looked down on the body of Bilotti, Gravano said to Gotti, "He's gone."

Hearing the shooting going on outside, DeCicco, Failla and Marino quickly left the restaurant. As they hurried down 46th Street they ran into Thomas Gambino, Castellano's nephew, who was on his way to the Sparks' meeting.

"Your uncle's been shot," said DeCicco.

"Is he dead?" Gambino asked

"He is, so Tommy," DeCicco confirmed.

"Jesus, what's going on?" Gambino inquired.

"Don't worry, everyone else is okay. Get to your car and leave. We'll be in touch," DeCicco assured.

Crime scene photos from outside Spark's Steak House

Paul Castellano

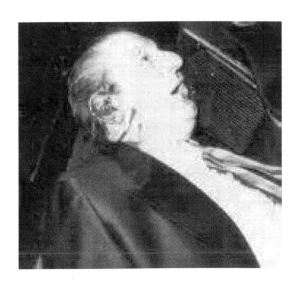

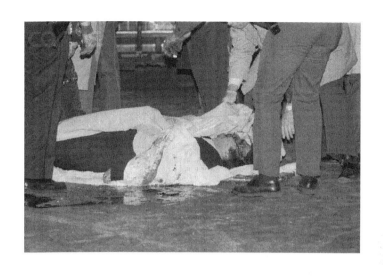

Tony Bilotti

Dec. 17, 1985 with headline detailing the mob hit of Paul Castellano

On December 24th At the Ravenite Social Club in Little Italy, Gotti receives the royal treatment from underlings after his ascension to Gambino family boss.

Part Two
Godfather of the Gambino Family

With Castellano, Bilotti and Dellacroce all gone, Gotti took control of the largest Mafia family in the nation, setting up his headquarters in the Ravenite Social Club.

Over the next few years, Gotti became a media hound. He paraded in his expensive suits and coats for the media, who always seemed to be there ready to take his picture.

Gotti demanded that the Family capos and soldiers come to the Ravenite to show their respect to him. This compromised many of them by exposing them to television coverage, a fact that late came back to haunt some of them.

The newly crowned boss of the Gambino Family was busy preparing for two trials. The first was for assaulting Romual Piecyk, a refrigerator repairman.

On September 11, 1984 the beefy looking, 6-foot-2 Piecyk, 35, found his car blocked by a double-parked automobile outside the Cozy Corner Bar in the Maspeth section of Queens. No stranger to criminal acts, Piecyk laid on his horn until the owner of the offending vehicle appeared. Frank Colletta, a Gambino Family associate, smacked Piecyk in the face and ripped $325--the repairman's weekly pay---from his shirt pocket. Piecyk jumped out of the car and began fighting with Colletta. Just then John Gotti exited the bar and entered the fray by slapping Piecyk across the face. Gotti then made a motion to withdraw something from his waistband, and as he did, he warned Piecyk, "You better get the f*** out of here."

Gotti and Colletta returned to the bar while Piecyk went to notify the police. He then returned to the Cozy Corner in the company of two officers, who arrested the two Gambino hoods. A few days later Piecyk testified before a grand jury. Gotti and Colletta were indicted and charged with felony assault and theft. More than a year would pass before the case came to trial. By that time, Gotti's face had been seen all over the newspapers and television in the wake of the Castellano/Bilotti murders.

With the trial approaching Piecyk was in fear for his life. He purchased a handgun and temporarily moved his pregnant wife out of their home. A week before the trial was to get under way, a sergeant from the Queens District Attorney's detective squad stopped at the Piecyk home to discuss the case.

"I ain't testifying," Piecyk told the sergeant.

In his report, the detective noted that Piecyk was afraid of Gotti's men. He had received anonymous phone threats and said the brakes on his work van had been cut. The threats prompted Queens District Attorney John J. Santucci to request an anonymous jury.

The trial, scheduled to begin March 2, 1986, was delayed five days while Justice Ann B. Dufficy considered, and then denied, the prosecution's request. On March 5, Piecyk spoke to a *New York Daily News* reporter. He denied receiving any threatening phone calls or having his vehicle tampered with. Piecyk then stated that he would appear as a witness for John Gotti.

"I am not going to go against Mister Gotti," he said. "I'm going in his behalf. I don't want to hurt Mister Gotti."

Testimony finally began on March 19. The next day when Piecyk was scheduled to take the stand, he didn't show. Members of Santucci's staff went to pick him up, but he could not be located. Despite his disappearance, law enforcement believed he had not met with foul play but rather was too scared to appear in court. Assistant District Attorney A. Kirke Bartley, Jr. told the judge that the prosecution was unable to proceed, due to the absence of the People's witness.

Late on Thursday, March 20, Piecyk was located at Mercy Hospital in Rockville Centre, Long Island. The reluctant witness had gone there to have elective surgery performed on his right shoulder, thinking that he could avoid having to testify. At Friday's court session, Bartley told Justice Dufficy that Piecyk would appear in court on Monday. Gotti's defense attorneys, who claimed that Piecyk had assaulted

Colletta and that their client had simply come to his aid, called the story a "sham." Bruce Cutler, appearing for the first time in defense of the soon-to-be christened "Dapper Don," claimed, "We don't know where he is, what hospital, who his doctor is."

Gotti's other attorney, Michael Coiro, Jr., who would later be found guilty of helping Angelo Ruggiero hide drug profits, told the court, "I think it's obvious the complaining witness is reluctant to testify."

On Saturday morning when Piecyk checked out of the hospital, detectives from the Queens district attorney's office took him into protective custody as a material witness. On Monday afternoon, sporting dark glasses and with his right arm in a sling, he took the witness stand to begin two hours of direct examination by prosecutor Bartley. In the hushed, packed courtroom in State Supreme Court in Queens, Piecyk was asked if he saw in the courtroom the men who had assaulted him.

"I do not," Piecyk replied.

When pressed to describe the men who had assaulted him, Piecyk stated, "To be perfectly honest, it was so long ago I don't remember." He claimed that his pocket had been ripped and his cigarettes and money taken, but he could not recall what had happened beyond that.

With this testimony, Justice Dufficy declared Piecyk a "hostile witness" and the trial was recessed. On March 25, prosecutor Bartley tried to resurrect the case by asking to introduce Piecyk's grand jury testimony. Dufficy denied the request and dismissed the assault and robbery charges against the two defendants. The *New York Daily News* printed its famous headline, "I FORGOTTI" in front page trial coverage. The Queens district attorney's office considered filing perjury charges against Piecyk but ultimately declined.

Yet this was not the last to be heard from Romual Piecyk. On August 27, 1986, during the jury selection for Gotti's RICO trial, prosecuted by Giacalone, Piecyk appeared at the Federal Courthouse in Brooklyn. After being denied the opportunity to speak in the courtroom, Piecyk held an impromptu press conference outside the courthouse. He told reporters that Gotti was being treated unfairly by the media, who had portrayed him as a "human monster."

Piecyk's appearance coincided with an affidavit he'd prepared for Gotti's lawyers that admitted the mob boss had never threatened or intimidated him. These actions took place after Gotti had been denied bail. In that decision, Federal Judge Eugene H. Nickerson had cited the fact that Piecyk had been "frightened" into changing his mind during Gotti's assault trial.

The Piecyk assault trial, the first of four trials, was over. The second trial, Giacalone's RICO trial, was scheduled to begin on April 7, 1986 just two weeks after the conclusion of the Piecyk case. Meanwhile, the basis for the third trial---the assault of a carpenter's union official---commenced with the wounding of John F. O'Connor on May 7, 1986.

Giacalone RICO Trial

Round One

No sooner had John Gotti returned from his Florida vacation (and celebration) in the Piecyk trial than he was back in court. On April 7, 1986, jury selection began in the Giacalone RICO trial. In addition to Gotti and his crew – Brother Gene, John Carneglia, Anthony Rampino and Willie Boy Johnson – Gambino Family members Nicholas Corozzo and Leonard DiMaria were being prosecuted.

Missing from the case were the Dellacroce's, father and son. Neil had passed away the previous December, and Armond had disappeared.

Armond Dellacroce had told his lawyer he was not up to standing trial and pled guilty on December 6, just four days after his father died. This decision upset Gotti. Although he was not going to testify against the others, the fact that Armond pled guilty to the same counts the others were charged with did not reflect well on the group. Gotti let it be known, "No matter how good a deal a prosecutor might offer, no member of the Gambino family could ever admit in a plea agreement that it (the family) existed." In April 1988, after being a fugitive for two years, Armond Dellacroce died of a cerebral hemorrhage brought on from acute alcohol poisoning in the Pocono Mountains area of Pennsylvania.

Also missing were John Carneglia's brother, Charles, who was officially listed as a fugitive, and William Battista, who Giacalone was going to call as a government witness. The seven defendants were accused of Federal racketeering charges and racketeering conspiracy counts. The indictments listed criminal acts that took place over an 18-year period. All the men were looking at prison terms of 20 years, in addition to stiff fines.

Because of the success Gotti had achieved intimidating Romual Piecyk; he decided to use the same tactics again. The first government witness to be approached was Dennis Quirk who was subpoenaed to testify regarding the 1976 murder of court officer Albert Gelb. The 25 year-old official, described as the "city's most decorated uniform court officer," had been murdered shortly before he was to testify against fugitive defendant Charles Carneglia. Giacalone told Federal Judge Eugene Nickerson that Gotti's people had tried to contact

Quirk on two occasions. The prosecutor told the judge she would move to have the defendants' bails revoked if any future contact were attempted with the government's witnesses. Nickerson agreed to keep the names of government witnesses secret until they testified, and ordered the defendants to steer clear of them.

On the morning of April 9, a bomb threat was telephoned into the courthouse, clearing it immediately. Gotti told a friend, "Tell them it's not me. They'll be blaming this one on me." He was partially correct. The man who made the call claimed he was John Gotti. It was later discovered the culprit was Alexander Galka, a hospitalized mental patient who was due in court that afternoon for sentencing for making threats against President Ronald Reagan.

Also on April 9, the two mob attorneys, Cutler and his one-time law partner Barry Slotnick, let the underworld know where their loyalties lay. The two withdrew from representing Joseph Colombo, Jr., and his brother Anthony, sons of the former mob boss of the Colombo Family.

Slotnick claimed that one of the former defendants in that case, Alphonse Merolla, had become a government witness. Merolla had been defended by Cutler, and the lawyers decided that any further representation in the trial would constitute a conflict of interest.

Four days later, Gambino Family underboss Frank DeCicco was murdered in a sensational car bombing. The trial was not yet a month old and it had already experienced missing defendants, a bomb scare, intimidation of witnesses and the murder of a high-ranking associate of the group. This was only the beginning of what would turn into a circus-like atmosphere and complete mockery of the justice system. On April 28, Judge Nickerson's decision to postpone the case came as no surprise. In announcing it, the judge had cited, "events of the past few weeks," his own observations during the jury selection process, and the extensive news coverage of the case, which had only intensified with the murder of DeCicco.

Bombed car of Frank DeCicco

Nickerson refused to elaborate, or to explain why he chose a four-month moratorium for the trial. Yet despite the postponement, Gotti's legal woes weren't over. Prosecutor Giacalone moved to have Gotti and three other defendants' bails revoked, claiming they had "violated the conditions of their release" and "continued participation in the activities of the Gambino organized-crime family." Several witnesses testified during the three days of hearings. Lieutenant Remo Franceschini, commander of the Queens' District Attorney's detective squad, testified that his informants had said that Gotti was "involved in illegal activities, including gambling and shylocking."

John Gurnee, who was an organized crime specialist with the New York Police Department's Intelligence Division and who had taken dozens of photographs of the mob boss and his associates, also testified. He told Judge Nickerson that while Gotti was out on bail, the new mob leader had received "unusual respect" from mobsters following the murder of Paul Castellano, and was "accorded even greater respect" at the wake of Frank DeCicco. Edward Magnuson, a supervising agent for the DEA, testified that a confidential informant had told him that Gotti was "very angry relative to the murder of Frank DeCicco, and when he was out on bail, or when the trial was over, there was going to be a war, and John would take his revenge."

After hearing from eleven government witnesses, prosecutors Giacalone and John Gleeson stated in a 40-page memorandum that if Gotti and the other defendants were allowed to remain free, "they would try to intimidate witnesses or jurors." On May 13, Judge Nickerson revoked John Gotti's bail, stating that there was substantial evidence that while out on bail, the mob boss had been involved in the intimidation of Romual Piecyk. Therefore Gotti was considered "reckless" and "dangerous" and "worthy of detention." Not even a Bruce Cutler-induced affidavit from Piecyk stating that he was "never harassed" could prevent the Dapper Don from being locked up. However, none of the other defendants were held, although prosecutors had requested it.

On May 19, 1986, after Cutler's arguments failed before a panel of three judges of the U.S. Court of Appeals for the Second Circuit, Gotti was searched, fingerprinted and photographed in Brooklyn's Federal Courthouse. He had arrived in a black Mercedes Benz and he left in a dirty blue Dodge prison van that was headed for the Metropolitan Correctional Center (MCC) in lower Manhattan. "Let's go," Gotti told his captors, "I'm ready for Freddy."

Chin's Retaliation

Vincent (Chin) Gigante

Before having Castellano murdered, Gotti had sought the approval of the other New York families, with the exception of the Genovese Family and their leader Vincent "the Chin" Gigante. After the murder, Gigante, who would soon be the only member of the Commission that wasn't dead or in prison, sought to avenge the killing. Gotti had sent a message to Gigante and the other families that "all was well" with the Gambino Family, and a message was relayed back from the Genovese boss that "someday, someone would have to pay for Paul."

In *Gotti: Rise and Fall*, the authors reveal Gigante's plan as he plotted with old-time Gambino capos, James "Jimmy Brown" Failla and Daniel Marino. Failla controlled the city's private sanitation industry and Marino was a trucking-company proprietor. Capeci and Mustain write:

"He (Gigante) also intended to play kingmaker. After Gotti and DeCicco were dead, he would step in and urge the Gambino capos to elect Failla, who had been a friend as long as Paul was. Failla, at his urging, would then choose Marino...as his underboss."

Gotti and DeCicco had made a point of visiting the various family capos on their home ground, something Castellano considered beneath him. On Sunday, April 16, 1986, just days after the Giacalone RICO trial began, Gotti was supposed to meet DeCicco and Gravano at Failla's Veterans & Friends social club in Benson Hurst. In addition to crewmembers of Failla, Danny Marino was also in attendance.

Outside the club, several hundred yards away, a hit team that was organized by Gigante and Lucchese Family higher-up Anthony "Gas Pipe" Casso was ready for action. A bomb hidden in a brown bag was placed under DeCicco's automobile. What the killers didn't know was that Gotti had telephoned the club earlier to let them know he couldn't make it and for DeCicco to meet him later that day at the Ravenite.

While members of the group were discussing family business, Frank Bellino, a member of the Lucchese Family, arrived to discuss a legal problem with DeCicco. Bellino wanted the telephone number of an attorney and DeCicco had the lawyer's business card in the glove compartment of his Buick Electra. As the two men approached the car DeCicco commented about a bag that was visible under the vehicle. "There's probably a bomb under my car," he joked to Bellino.

As the two men approached the car, Herbert "Blue Eyes" Pate, an associate of the Genovese Family (who years later was ratted out by Anthony Casso as the hit man), was given a signal. He waited as DeCicco sat down on the passenger's side and opened the glove compartment. Then he detonated the bomb. Gang members, except Failla and Marino, rushed from the social club to the scene of carnage. Gravano pulled his dying friend away from the burning automobile. Both victims were taken by a police van to Victory Memorial Hospital, where DeCicco was pronounced dead. Gotti moved quickly to gather the troops. All of the family capos and their crewmembers were ordered to attend the wake for a showing of strength and unity.

Unaware of who was behind the murder, Gotti still believed he had a good working relationship with Gigante. The Chin thought otherwise and was not finished with his effort to remove Gotti from the leadership of the Gambino Family. However, according to Gravano, Gigante wasn't the only one plotting. In 1988, Gotti requested a meeting of the Commission. With his friend Joseph Massino (head of the Bonanno Family but removed years earlier from his Commission seat), Gotti lobbied to get the Bonanno boss back on the Commission. Then in a power play, Gotti backed Vic Orena for the position of "acting boss" of the Colombo Family. Gotti's game plan was that, with the loyalty of those two family bosses, he could control the Commission.

As the maneuverings raged on, a New Jersey faction of the Genovese Family was making plans to kill both John Gotti and his brother Gene. Louis Anthony "Bobby" Manna, a 59-year-old capo from

Jersey City, conspired with five other gang members to pull off the assassination. When government agents heard about the plot from listening devices planted in the restaurant of Martin "Motts" Casella, they notified Gotti. In June 1989, Manna and two others were convicted in the death plot.

Giacalone RICO Trial

Round Two

Attorney Bruce Cutler (left) with John Gotti

A month prior to the trial reconvening, Bruce Cutler was back in the courthouse requesting that his client be allowed to come to his office each morning to discuss trial strategy. "My client takes great pride in his appearance, as the court knows," Cutler told Judge Nickerson. Gotti was even willing to pay for the additional cost of being moved around by the Federal marshals. Prosecutor Giacalone opposed the motion on the grounds that it would create two classes of defendants – "one for those who can pay for special services and the other for those who cannot pay." Nickerson rejected the request.

Pretrial motions were handled on August 18, 1986. Judge Nickerson had ruled that an anonymous jury would be impaneled to protect jurors from intimidation – and the jury would not be sequestered. Cutler claimed, "Such a jury creates an aura of fear that is misplaced and deprives the defendants of a fair trial." Defense attorneys then charged that Nickerson was biased. Other motions by the defense bordered on the absurd. They complained about pretrial publicity, seating arrangements – which gave the prosecution "better eye contact" with the jury – and where Gotti would be served lunch. After a series of motions were denied to have both Nickerson and Giacalone removed, jury selection got under way.

The jury panel consisted of 450 prospective jurors (some references list it as high as 600), from which 12 jurors and 6 alternates would be selected. When Nickerson convened the earlier trial, he stated that he would use different procedures this time to qualify prospective jurors. This new method, according to defense attorneys, could lead to a selection of jurors who were either "ignorant or inhibited." Cutler argued, "Anyone who can see or hear and has half a brain has to know about my client." Jury selection was completed after 18 days. Selection of the six alternates would take another week. The trial, which had been estimated to last 60 to 90 days, took nearly 40 days altogether to seat a jury.

On September 25, opening statements were delivered in the Federal District Court in Brooklyn. Assistant U.S. Attorney Diane Giacalone gave a 90-minute statement to the jury before an audience of approximately 100 people. At least a quarter of the spectators were reporters or sketch artists.

It is perhaps in Giacalone's first remarks that the myth of John Gotti murdering James McBratney to avenge the murder of Manny Gambino and ingratiate himself with Carlo Gambino was born. She claimed that his participation in the murder began his climb to prominence and leadership of the Gambino Crime Family. She asked the jury, "What sort of an organization is it where murder is a means of advancement?" Giacalone told the jury that they would be hearing testimony from witnesses that were murderers, drug dealers and kidnappers. "They're just horrible people," she warned. What an understatement this would prove to be!

Cutler responded in his opening remarks by claiming, "The only family John Gotti knows is his wife and children and grandchildren." The overly dramatic defense attorney pranced around the courtroom making disparaging comments about the prosecutor and the indictment. At one point he took the indictment and tossed it in a wastebasket stating, "It's garbage. That's where it belongs." Calling the government's witnesses "scum" and "lowlifes," the defense team claimed that their clients "were being prosecuted because of past misdeeds for which they had already served prison terms and because the Government did not like the way they lived."

The prosecution's case did not get off to a good start. Their first witness was to be Salvatore "Crazy Sal" Polisi. Saturday, two days before he was to testify, Polisi gave a taped interview to a writer who was doing a book about Polisi's life. (This project failed, but a later book, *Sins of the Father: The True Story of a Family Running from the Mob*, by Nick Taylor, would be published in 1989.) Because the rules of evidence state the defense is entitled to the same information about a prosecution witness that the prosecution has, in time to cross-examine the witness, Polisi's testimony was delayed. Instead the government played wiretap tapes and called Francis J. Leonard, a Suffolk County detective, who described an illegal numbers operation run by defendants DiMaria and Corozzo back in 1975.

On October 6, the *New York Times* published an article by Selwyn Raab in which the reporter stated that Gotti was "on his way out as boss of the Gambino organized-crime family, and potential successors are maneuvering to succeed him, according to law-enforcement experts on the Mafia."

Raab pointed out that the "experts'" reasoning was Gotti's legal problems and "the belief among influential Gambino family captains that he faces a long prison term." In addition, unnamed law enforcement officials claimed that additional indictments, on both the state and federal levels, were being sought. One federal official stated, "Everybody on the street is convinced he's going away for a long time, 20 years or more." Lieutenant Remo Franceschini said that Thomas Gambino was the person most likely to succeed Gotti. He added, "If Gotti is replaced, it will be by a low-key traditional organized-crime type." Raab summed up his article by stating that "law-enforcement officials said the Gambino group captains apparently were seeking a leader with a lifestyle less flamboyant that Mr. Gotti's." The Dapper Don, Raab claimed, was said "to have antagonized some factions in the Gambino family, as well as leaders of the other families, because of his penchant for notoriety."

Meanwhile the government was handed another setback on October 10, when they were told that the jury could not hear "key testimony" from Edward Maloney. The testimony was to establish a motive for the 1973 slaying of James McBratney. Nickerson accepted arguments from the defense that Maloney should not be allowed to testify about hearsay conversations he had not had with mob figures.

"I just think it is too thin," the judge stated. Maloney would be the first witness to get "Brucified," that is unmercifully ripped apart by the classless defense attorney, a term that the arrogant Cutler accepted with great pride. In describing Maloney's payments from the government, Cutler stated, "Put it this way, Mr. Maloney, that it cost the United States of America some fifty-two thousand dollars to give you a new identity, to give you a new home, to give you a new job, to cut your hair, and give you a suit, a menace and a bum like you."

Next to go into what Jerry Capeci termed the "defense shredder" was "Crazy Sal" Polisi. On October 15, Barry Slotnick manipulated the Blacks on the jury by pointing out that Polisi believed "that black people were the lowest form of humanity." Polisi insisted that he was a reformed man, to which Cutler dug in and inquired about "this new religion? Tell us so we can free the jails of lowlifes like you."

In addition to the comments that were directed at witnesses, several "under the breath" comments were made to the prosecution team by defense attorneys and defendants. In early November, former New York Police Department detective Victor Ruggiero was under cross-examination and was giving defense counsel Michael Santangelo a particularly hard time. Ruggiero (no relation to Angelo) was testifying about surveillance outside the Ravenite Social Club during 1978 and 1979.

When Santangelo questioned the judge about the witness's evasive answers, Nickerson addressed the former officer. "Why do you do that? The questions are very simple." Seated behind Giacalone, Gotti sarcastically remarked loud enough for the jury to hear, "He is doing that because they threatened him; that is why."

Giacalone immediately called for a sidebar and the jury was asked to step out. In a brief outburst, Gotti told the judge, "Your honor, it's not true."

"Don't make comments," Judge Nickerson scolded him.

"But it's not true, your honor," Gotti insisted. "If anybody is making comments, it's her."

The trial was falling under the guidelines for a "mockery of justice." Defense attorneys continued to slam government witnesses and defendants joked and made disgusting remarks behind the prosecutors' backs, most of them directed at Giacalone. Gotti made regular disparaging remarks to news reporters about the proceedings, which they ate up. Finally, control of the courtroom, by what could only be described as the milquetoast efforts of Judge Nickerson, was quickly evaporating.

John's Special Juror

The reason for Gotti and Cutler's being confident in beating the case was justified. They had bought a juror for $60,000. George Pape was described as a "middle-aged suburbanite with a drinking problem." While working at a construction site he'd met Bruno Radonjich, who would become the leader of the Westies Gang. When Pape was called for jury duty and realized he might sit on the Giacalone RICO case, he saw it as a financial opportunity.

Pape lied early and often in an effort to get through Judge Nickerson's questionnaire to eliminate potential jurors who could show any connection to Gotti. Soon after being accepted, Pape contacted Radonjich, who in turn "reached out" to Sammy Gravano, and the fix was on.

Gotti seemed to revel in the fact that the worst thing that could happen to him would be a hung jury. During trial recesses, he would give impromptu interviews to the media, which usually consisted of denouncing the prosecution, one of their witnesses, or both. On November 19, 1986, when the verdict came down in the famous "Commission" trial, convicting all eight defendants of RICO violations, Gotti let it be known that the decision had "nothing to do with us. We're walkin' out of here."

At times, the prosecutors proved to be their own worst enemy with some of the witnesses they called. In early December, former Bergen club hanger-on James Cardinali took the stand. Cardinali had been in prison with Gotti when he was serving time for the McBratney murder. Cardinali was serving a five- to ten-year term for murder when he became a government witness. He told the court that after leaving prison in 1979, he sought out Gotti at the Bergin and was given a no-show job at a trucking firm, paid $100 to $200 a week by Gotti to run errands. During this time he admitted to robbing drug dealers and killing five people. After Cardinali's first morning of testimony, Gotti told reporters in the spectator section, "Not one thing he said was the truth – except his rat name."

Under cross-examination, Cardinali embarrassed the government. Attorney Jeffrey C. Hoffman, representing Gene Gotti, got Cardinali to admit that the government paid him $10,000 for his testimony and when asked if he would "lie, cheat or steal" to get what he wanted he replied,

"Absolutely!" Over the prosecutor's objections, Hoffman then dug into Cardinali's conversations with Giacalone. He asked about comments Giacalone made about her working relationship with Judge Nickerson.

"Did you ever say that she said he treats her like a daughter?" Hoffman questioned. "And that she gets whatever she wants from him and that the defense gets nothing?"

"I heard something like that," Cardinali replied.

Under questioning from defense attorney Michael L. Santangelo, who represented Leonard DiMaria, Cardinali admitted that, in addition to the money, he'd been promised immunity in four murders in which he'd participated and would be given a new identity and home.

 When asked if he felt he had made a good deal with the government, Cardinali replied, "I think I made a fantastic deal."

By the sixth day of his testimony, Cardinali was sounding more like a defense witness than a government one. Cutler got him to admit he had once stated, "From the day I met John Gotti he did nothing but good for me. He put money in my pocket when I didn't have a dime, he put clothes on my back. He is the finest man I have ever known." The following day he admitted that he told Cutler, "If he [Gotti] found me and left me dead in the street, that's what I deserved."

Perhaps the most damaging revelation was Cardinali testifying that in 1982 he offered government agents information about an associate "who made millions dealing in drugs." Cardinali claimed the agents responded that they didn't need him for that, "they wanted John."

The trial, which was expected to last up to three months, dragged on into the new year. By January 20, 1987, five months after jury selection began, the defense finally began its case.

If Giacalone and Gleeson thought the worst was over, they were sadly mistaken. On February 2, defense witness Matthew Traynor took the stand and proceeded to spew sordid tales of alleged arrangements between the prosecutor and himself. The stories ranged from him being offered drugs in exchange for testimony to a repugnant tale of Giacalone offering Traynor a pair of her panties so he could "facilitate" himself after telling her he wanted to "get laid."

Traynor claimed that DEA Supervisor Magnuson provided him with drugs while in prison and that one time he was so "zonked" that he puked on Giacalone's desk. The defense left no prosecutor unscathed, as a subpoena was served on the hospital records of John Gleeson's wife. The defense tried to tie in the drugs Traynor was receiving to the wife of the prosecutor, who worked at the hospital.

On February 11, the defense rested its case. To Nickerson's chagrin, Giacalone announced that she had 17 rebuttal witnesses to call. The trial dragged on for three more weeks. On March 2, Giacalone spent five hours giving her summation. The once determined prosecutor looked beaten. Her voice was nearly gone and several times she misidentified people.

After a trial that lasted nearly seven months, the jury deliberated for seven days and then came to its decision. The prosecution was in a no-win situation. From the first day of deliberations it was a foregone conclusion, as George Pape announced to his fellow jurors that, "This man Gotti is innocent. They are all innocent. As far as I am concerned there is nothing left to discuss." Several jurors urged Pape to continue to deliberate and keep an open mind. Over the next few days they continued their work, mostly without him. At night Pape remained alone and drank by himself. In *Gotti: Rise and Fall*, Capeci and Mustain write:

"As some jurors later recalled, some began to suspect that somehow the defendants had threatened Pape or his family. This suspicion heightened the sense of danger that some had felt in the stares of Gotti and his men from the first day of trial and made them dwell on their own families' security. Over the last two days of deliberation, an unspoken group paranoia took hold and the tide turned the other way, creating a beach of reasonable doubt upon which early beliefs in the strength of the government case were gradually discarded."

On Friday the 13th, when the not guilty verdicts were announced, a raucous response from the Gotti faithful reverberated throughout the courtroom. His supporters actually believed he had won the trial, fair and square. As the jury began to exit, Gotti began clapping for them and was soon joined by his fellow defendants and supporters.

There are a few footnotes to the Giacalone RICO trial. Exactly one month after the verdict "Crazy

Sal" Polisi had his 15-year sentence reduced to probation. On the morning of August 29, 1988 mob justice was administered to Willie Boy Johnson. As Johnson walked from his Flatlands' home in Brooklyn to his car, gunmen fired nineteen rounds at him. Johnson was hit once in each thigh, twice in the back, and at least six times in the head. He died instantly. Finally in 1992, Sammy Gravano testified against juror George Pape, who was convicted and sent to prison for three years. Radonjich, who had fled to his homeland and became a Serbian freedom fighter, was arrested at Miami International Airport on New Year's Day, 2000. Gravano was expected to testify against him, but after Sammy was arrested on drug charges in late February, the government dropped its charges against Radonjich.

The Wounding of John O'Connor

In February 1986, the Bankers and Brokers Restaurant in Battery Park City was under construction. The restaurant was "under the management" of Philip Modica, whom police described as a "Gambino crime-family soldier." Modica was not using union carpenters in the construction, which incurred the wrath of John F. O'Connor, 50, the business agent and chief operating officer of Manhattan-based Local 608 of the United Brotherhood of Carpenters & Joiners. O'Connor responded by having the restaurant "trashed" one February night, causing some $30,000 worth of damage.

When Modica took his complaint to Gotti, the Gambino crime boss ordered that O'Connor be "busted up" and the assignment was given to members of the "Westies," a gang of Irish thugs from the Hell's Kitchen section of Manhattan. At 6:40 on the morning of May 7, O'Connor was waiting to enter an elevator in the lobby of a midtown Manhattan building that housed his union offices. Westies' gang member Kevin Kelly shot four times at O'Connor, wounding him in the buttock, left leg and hip. The union official was rushed to St. Clare's Hospital, where he soon recovered.

On September 23, 1986, O'Connor was arraigned for coercion and criminal mischief in the damaging of the restaurant. Charged the same day was the gunman who'd wounded him---who at the time was a fugitive. Information had been supplied to the Manhattan District Attorney, Robert M. Morgenthau, by the former number two man in the Westies, now government witness, Francis "Mickey" Featherstone.

Nearly two years and four months would pass before Morgenthau's office would indict Gotti for first degree assault and conspiracy in the fourth degree for the attack on O'Connor. On January 24, 1989, Gotti was arrested in the late afternoon as he walked along a Soho street. Thrilled to be making the arrest was State Task Force officer Joseph Coffey. The former New York Police Department detective, who openly referred to the Gambino Crime Family boss as a moron, almost slammed Gotti through a plate glass window before handcuffing him.

The cocky mob boss told Coffey, "I'll lay you three to one I beat it."

"Forget it, jerkoff, get in the fucking car," replied Coffey.

Also arrested that night on the same charges were Angelo Ruggiero and Anthony "Tony Lee" Guerrieri. Ruggiero was placed under arrest at New York Infirmary-Beekman Hospital in Manhattan, where he was receiving cancer treatments. He passed away before the trial got under way. Guerrieri ran an illicit bookmaking enterprise for Gotti. His rap sheet included a number of arrests for gambling and receiving stolen goods. Although convicted several times, he'd never been sent to prison.

During his arraignment Gotti sat and joked with detectives. When he was placed in the detention cell behind the courtroom, about 50 defendants got to their feet and applauded him. Attorney Bruce Cutler pleaded with the judge not to make Gotti spend the night in jail.

Assistant District Attorney Michael Cherkasky stated, "Mr. Gotti needs to be treated like any other defendant." To which Cutler responded, "If Mr.

Gotti was like any other defendant, then they wouldn't have used 100 people to arrest him."

At the bail hearing the following day, Cherkasky urged the judge to ensure that Gotti be held without bail. The prosecutor stated that the boss of the Gambino Crime Family was looking at 25 years to life if convicted and had "enormous financial resources." Cutler told the judge that Gotti, "never ran away from a problem, never. We will win this case. We are not concerned." Gotti was released on $100,000 bond and while leaving the courthouse, he then fought his way through a sea of reporters, television cameramen and photographers.

The O'Connor Trial

Gotti kept talking and the FBI bugs kept recording. Listening devices were planted at the Bergin and the Ravenite. Agents monitored the mobsters whenever they met. One of the FBI's coups was the planting of bugs in Nettie Cirelli's apartment above the Ravenite, where Gotti felt completely safe to speak. Between November 30, 1989 and January 24, 1990, Gotti was to spill enough of the family's secrets to finally bring the walls crashing down.

While the listening devices in Cirelli's apartment continued to record damaging information leaking from the lips of the Gamino Family boss, his trial in the John O'Connor shooting was to begin in January 1990. Jury selection started on January 8 and was completed eleven days later. Acting Supreme Court Judge Edward J. McLaughlin ordered the jury to be sequestered for the entire trial and, to speed the proceedings, ordered that sessions be scheduled for six days a week.

The prosecution had two informants and mountains of tapes, the most damaging of which they claimed Gotti was overheard ordering, "Bust him up!" The first witness called by the prosecution was Vincent "Fish" Cafaro, a Mafia turncoat and a former made member of the Genovese Crime Family. Cafaro had been called by the state to testify as to how the five New York crime families operated. Gotti defense lawyers Cutler and Shargel tried to discredit Cafaro's testimony. Cutler inquired as to how the witness received his nickname, "Fish"?

"I don't recall," Cafaro replied.

"It has nothing to do with an odor or slipperiness?" Cutler asked sarcastically.

Next up for the jury were the tape recordings from the listening devices planted by members of the New York State Organized Crime Task Force. One agent described how he'd picked the lock to a door that led them into Gotti's private office, which was next to the Bergin Hunt & Fish Club where they planted bugs in two of the mob boss's telephones.

Quick to arise was the fact that if the authorities knew that O'Connor was in danger, why didn't they warn him? One investigator testified under cross-examination that the tapes weren't clear enough for them to identify O'Connor. Outside the courtroom, Gotti defense attorney Shargel told reporters, "If the tapes weren't clear enough to warn O'Connor, then they are not clear enough to convict Gotti."

On January 24, Edward Wright, an investigator for the State Organized Crime Task Force, testified for three hours about the content of the tapes. Explaining the tape's "cryptic references," Wright outlined for the jury the structure and titles of mob family members.

The star witness for the prosecution was former Westies gang member James Patrick McElroy, who was convicted in 1988 in Federal court of racketeering charges, including the assault on John O'Connor. It was only after McElroy agreed to cooperate with the government in 1988 that an indictment against Gotti was issued. McElroy was sentenced from 10 to 60 years in federal prison and was admittedly looking for a reduction of that sentence in return for his testimony.

He told the court the order to "whack" O'Connor came from Gotti through Westies' leader James "Jimmy" Coonan. Under questioning from prosecutor Cherkasky, McElroy admitted to murdering two men, shooting two others and cutting the throat of another.

McElroy claimed Coonan introduced him to Gotti at the wake of Frank DeCicco. While having dinner afterwards, Coonan told him that Gotti wanted someone whacked. A few weeks later, McElroy and Coonan met Angelo Ruggiero in Manhattan, where they were asked, "Can you handle it?" McElroy then testified that on the morning of May 7, 1986 he and Westies' gang members Kevin Kelly and Kenneth Shannon, along with gang hopeful Joseph Schlereth, met outside O'Connor's office building. After O'Connor entered the lobby, Schlereth shot him four times. "I saw him spinning around in circles," McElroy stated. "He was trying to get into the elevator."

During a grueling four-hour cross-examination on January 29, Cutler and Shargel ripped into McElroy. Judge McLaughlin had to admonish Cutler several times for his antics. Pounding the prosecution table, Cutler called McElroy a "stool pigeon" and a "yellow dog." At one point Cutler told the witness, "You know you never went to the wake. John Gotti is a man you don't know. You must have met him in one of your drunken and drugged dreams."

Near the completion of the cross-examination, McElroy stated that he hoped to join the Federal Witness Protection Program. Cutler barked, "You're looking to be plopped down in some unsuspecting community, like in Utah, where they never heard of you, and where you can cut more throats and do more drugs."

The following day the jury heard the famous, "We're gonna, gonna bust him up," line from Gotti on tape.

The prosecution contended this statement was made by Gotti to Guerrieri on February 7, 1986, just after the vandalism was done to the restaurant. Another recording made on May 7 had Gene Gotti talking to Ruggiero about hearing that O'Connor had been shot four times that morning.

The response from the defense was to challenge the authenticity of the tapes, stating that they may have been tampered with. They also pointed out that the sound quality was so poor that making an accurate transcript was impossible. The tapes could only be heard in the courtroom with the use of earphones. Gotti refused to listen and sat glaring at jury members as the tapes were played.

Edward Wright took the jury through the tapes. In cross-examining him about Gotti's, "Bust him up," comment, Cutler disputed that the word was "him" claiming that his client said "'em," a contraction for "them." Cutler said the comment was actually, "We're gonna, gonna bust 'em up," meaning to move people around. Cutler and Wright had the following exchange:

Cutler: *Do you know if that "bust 'em up" meant split them up?*
Wright: *Taken in the context of the whole conversation, I think it is fairly obvious what he meant.*
Cutler: *You can read his mind? Take a look at him over there. Tell me what he's thinking about?*
Wright: *I wish I knew.*

The defense began their case by pointing out inconsistencies with a tape recording that was made days after the wounding of O'Connor. In a meeting at Rikers' Island prison, turncoat Westies' member Mickey Featherstone discussed the shooting with gang member Kevin Kelly, while two hidden tape recorders were utilized. One tape was turned over to the United States Attorney's office in Manhattan and the other went to the District Attorney in Manhattan. At the federal trial involving McElroy, Kelly was identified as the shooter and convicted, while at Gotti's trial, McElroy testified that the gunman was Schlereth. Due to the differences in the transcripts of the two tapes, defense attorneys tried to convince jury members that the prosecution had altered the tapes.

As a surprise witness, the defense called shooting victim John O'Connor. The union official, who was facing a state labor racketeering trial within the week, told the court that he was picked up by investigators from the State Organized Crime Task Force the day before the shooting. O'Connor testified that he was never told his life was in danger or that anyone was going to bust him up.

The defense was attempting to prove that since the investigators had not warned O'Connor, they had no evidence that named him as the target of Gotti's "bust him up" comment. O'Connor also testified that there were "internal conflicts" within the union at the time he was wounded and that he had many enemies.

In the book *Underboss: Sammy the Bull Gravano's Story of Life in the Mafia*, by Peter Maas, Gravano talks about the wounding of O'Connor, and the trial:

"'They were just supposed to give this O'Connor a serious beating,' Sammy said. 'But a lot of the Westies were all fucked-up, drug addicts and drunks. And they end up shooting O'Connor in his legs and ass for whatever reason. So now when the D.A. eventually gets into this, it's a major thing.'

"Sammy had sent a message to O'Connor through the Westies that, all things considered, it wasn't such a good idea 'to testify against John.' O'Connor obliged. On the witness stand he swore that he didn't have the slightest idea who would want to harm him."

The last defense witness was a member of the carpenters' union who had testified at two previous federal trials. Ivar Mikalsen stated that he had identified Westies' member Kevin Kelly as the gunman, which conflicted with McElroy's testimony that Joseph Schlereth was the actual shooter.

During final arguments, which the newspapers described as "unusually rancorous summations," prosecutors and defense lawyers traded insults in front of the jury. The usually soft-spoken Cherkasky, in his final summation, addressed the defense's emphasis of John O'Connor testifying on behalf of John Gotti. Cherkasky told the jury, "I can understand why. If you get shot for breaking up a restaurant, what happens if you testify against him."

'The Teflon Don'

The newspapers reported peripheral stories that were going on during the trial. They discussed how courtroom guards gave Gotti the VIP treatment, clearing onlookers so the Dapper Don and his attorneys could move about the courthouse. One newspaper wrote that Gotti was "never unattended." Associates held umbrellas for him when it rained, while another aide stood ready with paper towels as he washed his hands in the men's room. Actors Tony LaBianco and Ray Sharkey attended parts of the trial. It was believed that one of them would portray the mob boss in an upcoming movie.

The jury panel, twelve jurors and four alternatives, had been sequestered for three weeks. The *New York Times* reported:

"Confined to an undisclosed hotel, the jurors eat and travel together, always under the watchful eyes of court guards. They are barred from meeting relatives and friends, and telephone conversations are monitored.

"Stories about the trial and organized crime are clipped from newspapers and magazines read by

the nine men and seven women. Watching television is permitted but news programs are blacked out. Jurors who take a walk or attend religious services are escorted by guards."

Deliberations did not go smoothly. At one point an unidentified juror sent a note to Judge McLaughlin claiming there was much dissension among the jurors. The note stated:

I FEEL WE HAVE A JUROR WHO HAS BROUGHT BIAS INTO THIS ROOM. PLEASE ADVISE. THIS JUROR HAS INDICATED THAT HE HAD SOME OPINION ON GUILT OR INNOCENCE BEFORE THE TRIAL STARTED.

McLaughlin called the jury in and spoke to them. Stating that deliberations are often difficult, he joked, "You can't get 12 New Yorkers to agree on anything." One former prosecutor pointed out that, "When a jury is sequestered there is always a risk of personality clashes and increased tensions. Such tensions can lead to deadlocks and deadlocks can lead to mistrials."

After the third day of deliberations ended, police searched a black Lincoln Continental parked outside the courthouse. They had received a call stating that guns were inside the car. They asked the driver, John "Junior" Gotti, to step out. All they found was an aluminum baseball bat.

On Friday, February 9, 1990, the jury returned with a verdict. After only one vote to reach a decision, they found Gotti and Guerrieri not guilty on four assault charges and two conspiracy counts.

Jurors who agreed to be interviewed stated they found little credibility in the prosecution's tapes and their star witness James McElroy.

The *New York Times* analyzed the verdict:

"However fearless the jurors themselves sounded afterward, some defense lawyers hypothesize that subliminal fear of the "Dapper Don," a man who appears to thumb his nose at the authorities with impunity, may have affected their deliberations. And that fear, they say, can only be exaggerated by three weeks sequestration."

As the verdicts were being read, the courtroom spectators began to applaud and one Gotti supporter shouted, "Yeah, Johnny." Judge McLaughlin stopped the foreman and warned, "Folks, anyone doing that again will not leave here for 30 days. If you think I'm kidding, I invite you to try."

When the courtroom was cleared, the jubilant Gotti was escorted out of the courthouse through a private elevator reserved for judges. Once on the street, Gotti raised his fist in triumph for the crowds of supporters standing behind police barricades. On Mulberry Street, the victory was greeted with cheers and celebratory fireworks. In Ozone Park, red and yellow balloons awaited Gotti's return.

On July 5, 1990, John F. O'Connor pled guilty to reduced charges in State Supreme Court in Manhattan. The now former Carpenter's union official, who had been charged in 1987 in a 127-count indictment, received a prison sentence of one to three years. During the months of plea bargaining that preceded his guilty plea, the charge that he directed the damaging of the Bankers and Brokers restaurant in Battery Park City was dropped. O'Connor's lawyer, James M. LaRossa, hoped that through a work-release program his client would be out in less than one year.

The Relentless Pursuit

In the three trials since 1986, the New York Police Department, the US Attorney's office in Brooklyn and the state's Organized Crime Task Force had all taken a shot at John Gotti. All had failed. The FBI was next. Special Agent Jules J. Bonavolonta, who was in charge of the bureau's organized crime and narcotics division in New York, was quick to point out that the FBI had not been involved in the three cases which led to acquittals and earned Gotti the title of the "Teflon Don."

"We have not yet brought a case against John Gotti," Bonavolonta stated. "When we do, he can take all the bets he wants, but he's going to prison."

This bold statement was made the day following Gotti's latest acquittal. The fact that law enforcement was 0 and 3 against the popular Mafia godfather was no reason for them to stop trying. The verdict in the O'Connor trial came on a Friday. As Gotti was planning a Florida vacation that weekend, federal and state prosecutors had already planned to meet the following Tuesday to discuss a strategy to indict Gotti for the murder of his predecessor, Paul Castellano.

From day one, Gotti had been the main suspect in the murder of Castellano. With recent information from Philip Leonetti, the former underboss of the Philadelphia crime family (whose testimony helped put his uncle, Nicodemo "Little Nicky" Scarfo, behind bars for life), law enforcement was set to strike again. This time they would be patient in putting the finishing touches on an airtight case.

In *Gotti: Rise and Fall* the authors discuss a meeting held a week after the O'Connor verdict:

"The meeting was called by Jules Bonavolonta, Mouw's boss; newly confident that Gotti was a goner because of the Ravenite tapes, he wanted every official and agency interested in Gotti to set aside ego and institutional pride and endorse a single RICO case against the Gambino administration."

With talk of another indictment of Gotti in the aftermath of the O'Connor acquittal, both of the mob boss's attorneys had comments for the media. Gerald Shargel stated, "They don't prosecute John Gotti with evidence, but with theories." Meanwhile, Cutler called the continued investigation vendettas and witch-hunts. Cutler had represented Gotti at all three trials. In the Piecyk trial the victim was too scared to testify; in the Giacalone RICO case a juror had been bought off; and in the latest acquittal John O'Connor testified for the defense after being threatened. Despite the real reasons behind the acquittals, the arrogant Cutler selfishly took credit for everything. The onetime prosecutor became so enamored of Gotti that he began dressing like the popular mob boss and taking on his mannerisms.

John Gotti knew it would only be a matter of time before law enforcement would indict him on new charges. Following his acquittal in the O'Connor trial, Gotti took time out to enjoy the wedding of his son, Junior, to Kim Albanese in an ornate ceremony in April 1990.

Over that summer, Gotti prepared his crime family for the next encounter, which he knew could find him behind bars for a year or more before a verdict would be reached. His inner circle was dwindling. Robert DiBernardo was murdered by Gravano's men in June 1986. The killing of "DiB" was ordered by Gotti, probably at the insistence of Angelo Ruggiero, who owed DiBernardo a large sum of money and convinced John that his friend was talking "subversive" behind his back. In December 1987, Joseph "Piney" Armone and

Joseph N. Gallo were convicted, along with two others in the "Hierarchy" case. Both were sentenced to long prison terms. In 1992, Armone died at the Federal Medical Center in Springfield, Missouri.

Also gone were Gene Gotti and John Carneglia. After two mistrials they were finally found guilty of drug charges in a case dating back to 1983. On May 23, 1989, after a bizarre day of deliberations, both men were found guilty of running a multi-million dollar heroin ring. Said to be one of the oldest cases on the Federal dockets, a few hours before the verdict was reached a juror was dismissed after claiming he had been threatened in his driveway and feared for his and his family's lives. The jury continued with only eleven members. When they reached a decision, they walked back to the courtroom, only to be told by Judge John R. Bartels to go back and continue deliberations. This highly unusual move surprised both prosecutors and the defense counsel. On July 7, Gene Gotti and John Carneglia were sentenced to 50 years in prison and were each fined $75,000. A final appeal for the two men was turned down in March 1991.

Finally in December 1989, Angelo Ruggiero died of cancer. Gravano reported that during the last months of Ruggiero's life both Sammy and Gene Gotti urged John to visit his dying pal. Gotti refused to see his once loyal sidekick because he was still angry about all the grief he had caused by being caught on tape. Gravano claimed he nearly had to drag Gotti to the wake.

Meanwhile, despite the efforts of Jules Bonavolonta, a rift arose between three agencies wanting to prosecute the Teflon Don. Andrew Maloney, US Attorney for the Eastern District of New York won out over Otto Obermaier, who represented the Southern District, and the Manhattan District Attorney, Robert M. Morgenthau, who wanted a second shot at Gotti in the wake of the O'Connor failure. The decision came from Washington, D.C. in November 1990.

Gotti's Last Arrest

On the night of December 11, 1990 FBI agents and New York City detectives swooped down on the Ravenite social club and arrested Gotti, Sammy Gravano and Frank Locascio. Thomas Gambino was also arrested, but at another location. Following his arrest, the *New York Times* published an editorial that would show that sympathy for the mob boss went beyond his hired cronies. The editorial read in part:

"They arrested John Gotti the other night the same way they arrested him before, flamboyantly and theatrically...why all the melodrama, including handcuffs and a platoon of 15 FBI agents? The only obvious purpose is for the prosecution to preen for the cameras.

"Angered by the *Times* editorial, James M. Fox, the assistant director of the FBI's New York office replied in a letter that did not appear until January 19, 1991. The note pointed out that while it was true 15 law enforcement officers were dispatched to make the arrest, Gotti was surrounded by 26 underlings; only one photographer (from the New York Post) was present; that every FBI prisoner is handcuffed in compliance with regulations; the federal government was only involved in one previous arrest of Gotti.

Although this was the fourth indictment since Gotti's bloody rise to leadership, it was the first time he was charged with the murders of Castellano and Bilotti. Bolstering the government's claim in these accusations would be the testimony of Philip Leonetti, the former underboss of the Philadelphia Crime Family. Leonetti had become a government witness and was prepared to testify that Gotti bragged at a meeting of Philadelphia crime leaders that he had ordered Castellano's execution.

A week after the arrests, defense attorney Gerald Shargel was in court requesting that the tapes from the Cirelli apartment be kept from the public, claiming they would damage the defendant's right to a fair trial. Shargel told Judge Leo Glasser that the three defendants (Gambino had been released on bail) were confined to their cells for 24 hours a day, interfering with their right to meet with counsel.

Four days before Christmas 1990, Judge Glasser denied bail for Gotti and the other two men, claiming, "There are no conditions of release that will reasonably assure the safety of any person in the community." Meanwhile, after months of arguing between law enforcement agencies as to who would prosecute the case, a new controversy arose when it was revealed that the tapes had recorded Gotti discussing fixing the jury in the O'Connor trial. Morgenthau, whose office lost the case, was enraged that this information, recorded during the trial, was not brought to his attention until a year later. The Manhattan district attorney claimed the information could have led to a mistrial or separate state charges of jury tampering. The FBI's response to withholding the information included the possibility that the "disclosure of the bugging might have compromised" their investigation and subsequent indictment.

On January 18, 1991 Judge Glasser ordered an MCC official to end the "punitive conditions" under which the three defendants were forced to exist, which included 23-hour lockdowns. The official pointed out that the "administrative detention" was in part due to the judge's denial of bail, because of the violent charges against them. Judge Glasser responded that his directive was intended to protect the outside community, "not the population at the MCC."

At the same hearing Prosecutor John Gleeson presented a sealed motion to remove defense attorneys Bruce Cutler, Gerald Shargel and John Pollok from the case, claiming that they were caught on the Ravenite tapes and could be called as witnesses to testify. Judge Glasser gave the defense three weeks to respond. Leaving the courthouse, Cutler told reporters, "We're optimistic that we're going to remain as lawyers for these men."

On February 22, the three defense attorneys, represented by counsel, appeared before Judge Glasser. Gleeson presented several tape recordings from Gotti's Ravenite headquarters. Calling the lawyers "house counsel" for the Gambino Crime Family, Gleeson played a tape where Gotti complained, "Where does it end, the Gambino Crime Family?

This is the Shargel, Cutler and who-do-you-call-it crime family." Gleeson claimed the three should be disqualified, not only because their taped conversations were evidence but also because the tapes "raised a specter of improper conduct." The prosecutor further argued that "the lawyers had conflicts of interest because they had previously represented other defendants who could be witnesses in the Gotti trial." One tape had Gotti calling the lawyers "high-priced errand boys." After his court appearance Cutler stated, "We are proud of the way we have represented these men."

Despite the fact that Gotti was behind bars and could possibly remain there for the rest of his life, Vincent Gigante and Anthony Casso were still seeking revenge for the murder of Castellano. Just weeks before Gotti's arrest, Edward Lino, one of the shooters at Sparks Steak House, was gunned down. On April 13, Bartholomew "Bobby" Boriello, a close friend, confidant and chauffeur to both John Gotti and his son, Junior, was murdered outside his Bath Beach home in Brooklyn. In each killing, Gotti was unaware that it was a Gigante plot.

Federal prosecutors won a tactical victory on July 26, when Judge Glasser disqualified Cutler, Shargel and Pollok from representing the defendants. The defense lawyers claimed the taped conversations fell under the attorney-client privilege, but Glasser disagreed. One legal expert reviewing the judgment said the decision was "not common." The trial's commencement, scheduled to for September 23, was now in doubt (it would eventually be rescheduled for January 21).

On June 2, after constant pressure from the news media, Judge Glasser unsealed the FBI tapes of conversations recorded in the Ravenite, the club's hallway, and from the Cirelli apartment. Gotti's recorded conversations with Frank Locascio and Sammy Gravano spilled out into the newspapers and onto the six o'clock news. Included in these gems were the private conversations between Gotti and Locascio about Gravano, which would later lead to his defection.

In early August, Gotti, Gravano and Tommy Gambino appeared before Judge Glasser. The judge wanted to know if they had obtained new counsel. Gotti whined about having Cutler removed from the case. Calling Gleeson a "bum," Gotti stated, "He can't handle a good fight, and he can't win a fair trial." When Glasser asked Gravano if he had a new lawyer, Sammy responded with an incredulous, "In five days? It took six months to get rid of my lawyer, and you give me five days to find a new one? From the MCC, that's pretty hard." Glasser gave the men another week and told them he might consider appointing counsel if they didn't have representation by then.

There was much speculation as to who would take the case. Names being thrown around included F.

Lee Bailey, Albert Krieger, Jay Goldberg, Benjamin Brafman, James LaRossa, William Kunstler and Alan Dershowitz. When asked by reporters if he were interested, Kunstler replied, "No lawyer worth his or her salt should take this case while Gotti's being deprived of Bruce Cutler. It's wrong, politically and legally. But someone will succumb to the money or the publicity or both."

Some lawyers, speaking anonymously, didn't want to touch the case, due to Gotti's demeaning attitude towards attorneys.

In addition, Gotti had been recorded on tape bragging about how he had made the careers of both Cutler and Shargel. Once, when he was upset with Shargel, Gotti stated that he had "a better way than an elevator" to show Shargel out of the attorney's law office, which happened to be on the 32nd floor of an office building on East 58th Street. On August 20, Gotti selected Albert J. Kreiger as his attorney and Benjamin Brafman to represent Gravano. Thomas Gambino would be severed from the case and tried separately.

Against the objections of defense counsel Judge Glasser ordered that the jurors in the case would be sequestered and their names kept secret to "protect the integrity" of the trial. Along with this setback, the defense counsel had a more pressing issue to deal with – the defection of Salvatore "Sammy the Bull" Gravano on November 8, 1991.

Gotti's right-hand man, Salvatore "Sammy the Bull" Gravano, fires his lawyer and signs on as a government witness; testifies against Gotti.

Gotti's Final Trial

On the first day of jury selection, January 20, 1992, the prosecution called for the removal of another Gotti defense team member. George L. Santangelo, who was representing Frank Locascio, was accused by the government of being another of Gotti's "house counsel." The defense reacted by seeking the removal of John Gleeson, claiming he had "an intense personal interest in the case" due to losing the earlier RICO trial. When Glasser ruled in favor of the prosecution and removed Santangelo, Locascio pointed to the flag behind the judge's bench and shouted, "That's the American flag – not a swastika!" Santangelo was replaced by Anthony M. Cardinale.

As the jury selection process got under way, approximately 500 prospective jurors were handed a 21-page questionnaire to complete. A week later, while the selection was still going on, prosecutors asked the judge to limit the cross-examination of three government witness by the defense. The prosecution was trying to prevent the defense from "inflaming the jury" by having the witnesses describe the graphic details of the murders they were involved in. The three witnesses were

Gravano, Philip Leonetti and Peter Chiodo, a Genovese Family capo who had admitted involvement in four murders. During the trial, Chiodo's sister would become the target of mob hit men. She was wounded after returning home from dropping her children off at school.

One day while the completed questionnaires were being reviewed, Judge Glasser informed Gotti that flyers depicting Gravano as a "rat who lies" had been left on automobiles around the courthouse and in the neighborhood around the Ravenite. Glasser advised Gotti, "It might be a very good idea if you could put an end to it."

The jury selection proved to be a tedious one, as outside influences affected the process. Most of the problems were caused by the print media, who published what was supposed to be sealed information regarding six additional murders Gotti was rumored to be charged with. In addition, the *New York Post* published a headline article claiming that jurors were "petrified" of serving. In the courtroom on February 6, an irritated Judge Glasser let the defense know, "I am giving serious thought to moving the trial to another venue if this kind of media coverage and poisoning of the jury pool continues."

An angry Gotti, seated with his attorneys, waited for the judge to leave before blurting out, "Where is he going to move it, Stuttgart, West Germany?" Gotti then called the judge a faggot. Turning to the prosecution table, the well-coifed mob boss complained, "When was the last time those punks washed their hair?"

On February 11, a jury was finally seated and on the following day, the opening statement by US Attorney Andrew Maloney was delivered. Maloney told the jury, "This is not a complex case. These defendants will tell you in their own words what it's about." In describing Gravano's anticipated appearance, the prosecutor stated, "He is no different and no better than John Gotti." He then broke the news to the jurors that Gravano had been involved in 19 murders.

Defense attorneys Krieger and Cardinale delivered their opening remarks on February 13. Krieger began by apologizing for his client for the language the jurors were going to be subjected to on the government's tapes, claiming Gotti had grown up on the streets and that, "he learned to speak what they speak." While the lawyer admitted that profanity laced every sentence, he assured the jurors that, "It never intruded on his conversations with women and children." Of Gravano, Krieger described the government's key witness as "a little man full of evil...cunning, conniving, selfish and greedy...who has tried to clear his slate by admitting to 19 murders."

The early days of the trial were taken up by the testimony of FBI Agents George Gabriel and Lewis Schiliro, who described the Gambino Crime Family organization to jurors and explained the various audio and video tapes from the Ravenite Club surveillance. On February 19, Deena Milito testified. Fighting back tears, she described her relationship with her father Louis Milito, whose body was never recovered after he disappeared on May 8, 1988. Prosecutors claimed Gotti ordered his death. Also called to the stand was Jack Zorba a gambler whose small operation was closed after a pointed message, caught on tape was, was delivered to him, "You tell this punk, I, me, John Gotti, will sever his mother-fuckin' head off."

The jury next heard in Gotti's own words how he told Locascio about how he had ordered the murders of Robert DiBernardo, Louis Milito and Louie DiBono. This conversation had been recorded in the Cirelli apartment above the Ravenite on December 12, 1989. It was this tape, where Gotti blamed Gravano for requesting these murders, which chased Sammy into becoming a government witness. Gotti's defense lawyers tried to elicit from FBI Agent Schiliro that the mob boss did not speak with "Churchillian" eloquency and used exaggerations routinely in his speech.

During the last week of February, the prosecution slowly put their case together on the Castellano murder charge. Beginning with the tapes, where Angelo Ruggiero is caught discussing heroin sales with Gene Gotti and John's former attorney Michael Coiro, the prosecution moved on to talk about Castellano's ruling on drugs.

This sets the scene for Gotti to want to murder the Gambino Family boss to save his brother and friend Angelo. Two witnesses then testified that they saw John Carneglia and Anthony Rampino, associates of John Gotti, in front of Sparks Steak House the evening of the shooting. Both witnesses kept what they saw a secret for over a year and a half after the killing, out of fear for their lives.

On Monday, March 2, 1992 the moment everyone anticipated arrived: Salvatore "Sammy the Bull" Gravano was sworn in.

There are three side notes to events that took place while Gravano's testimony was going on. On March 3, the trial was interrupted when an elderly woman let out a mournful wail in the courthouse corridor. Anna Carini said she had come to spit in the face of Gravano because she held him responsible for the deaths of her two sons, Enrico and Vincent. The two, however, did not appear on Sammy's hit list. The following day, Judge Glasser dismissed two jurors. Although Glasser sealed the record on his decision, it was rumored that one, a 20 year-old man, asked to be dismissed because his girlfriend was frightened. Finally, as in an earlier Gotti trial, a bomb threat was called in which temporarily halted the proceedings.

The prosecution's case after the Gravano testimony was anti-climactic. Videos were shown to back up much of Gravano's claims and then prosecutors moved forward to bolster the other charges in the indictment. Chief among these was the obstruction of justice charge involving New York Police detective William Peist, who through Gambino associate George Helbig provided intimate details of the police intelligence department's activities to the mob.

During this stretch in the case, additional audiotapes were played, including conversations that included attorneys Gerald Shargel and Bruce Cutler. The last charge the prosecution covered was a count to defraud the government. Called to the stand was an IRS supervisor who testified that Gotti had not filed taxes for the previous six years.

Near the end of the prosecution's case, the defiant and arrogant attitude that Gotti had expressed during previous trials spilled out, and Judge Glasser admonished him.

The judge interrupted the testimony of a witness, ordered the jury out of the courtroom and then stood and glared down at Gotti from the bench. "Mr. Gotti, this is addressed to you. If you want to continue to remain at this trial and at that table, I am going to direct you to [stop] making comments which can be heard in this courtroom, [and making] gestures which are designed to comment upon the character of the United States attorney," the judge sternly said, "I will have you removed from the courtroom. You will watch this trial on a television screen downstairs. I am not going to tell you that again."

On March 23, amid yet another bomb threat to the Brooklyn Federal Courthouse, Andrew Maloney announced that the government was resting its case. The long awaited Gotti defense was a total shambles. The only defense witness lawyers were permitted to call was a tax attorney who claims he advised Gotti not to file tax returns while under indictment. Five other witnesses were ruled ineligible for a number of reasons, causing an outburst from attorney Cardinale that resulted in a contempt charge issued by Glasser. "What happened to our defense?" a disappointed Gotti inquired. "I should have put on a little song and dance."

John Gleeson began the government's summation on March 27, telling the jury that the combined evidence – Gotti's taped words and Gravano's testimony – provide "absolutely overwhelming evidence" to convict John Gotti. Describing the "Dapper Don" as the leader of the Gambino Crime Family, Gleeson stated, "Murder is the heart and soul of this enterprise."

Salvatore "Sammy the Bull" Gravano being sworn in

Both defense lawyers attacked Gleeson and Gravano in their summations. Cardinale described Gleeson's attitude as, "get Gotti at any cost" and claimed the prosecution's case was "nothing but a gloried frame-up." Krieger called Gravano a "sick serial killer," and said he delivered "John Gotti's head on a silver platter." Krieger told the jurors Gravano would receive a minimal sentence of no more than 20 years for his part in 19 murders as "long as he fulfilled his sick and distorted and manic promise to supply the testimony that you heard here."

On March 30, the prosecution gave its rebuttal summation. John Gleeson, who had handled the bulk of the prosecution's case, asked the jury to, "Look at all the evidence as a whole." He pointed out that during the defense's summations, they ignored the evidence and instead attacked him and Gravano.

In a move that almost proved disastrous U.S. Attorney Maloney completed the government's summation. He pointed to the defendants and told the jurors, "this is the leadership of the Gambino Crime Family. If you accept the proof of what you are dealing with here, the boss of a murderous and treacherous crime family and his underboss, you would be less than human if you didn't feel some personal concern."

Defense lawyers jumped to their feet, screaming objections, which Judge Glasser quickly sustained. After the jury left the courtroom defense attorneys angrily demanded a mistrial. Glasser rejected their demands.

The following day, after a third juror was dismissed at the request of the prosecution, Judge Glasser spent nearly four hours giving final instructions to the jury. As the day's court session ended, Gotti stood, pointed toward the prosecution table and called out to reporters, "the 1919 White Sox," indicating that the prosecutors had fixed the case.

The 'Velcro' Don

The jurors began their deliberations on the morning of Wednesday, April 1. After just 13 hours, the jury returned the following day, having found Gotti guilty of all the charges and Locascio guilty of all except one gambling count. James M. Fox, the assistant director in charge of the FBI's New York office, uttered his famous line, "The don is covered with Velcro, and every charge stuck." This was followed by Andrew Maloney's comment, "It's been a long road. Justice has been served and it feels awfully good." Meanwhile, prosecutor Gleeson told reporters, "We are very proud of what we've done. We have a great deal of admiration for a very courageous jury." Judge Glasser set his sentencing date for June 23.

The calls of guilty were not yet through ringing in the courtroom when the organized crime pundits were selecting a new boss for the Gambino Crime Family. The *New York Times* was already reporting that law enforcement authorities had revealed that 73-year-old capo James Failla was appointed acting boss by Gotti when he was arrested in December 1990. In addition to Peter Gotti and John's son, Junior, whom the "experts" claimed would not be good choices, other names being bandied around were Thomas Gambino, Joe Arcuri, Joseph "Butch" Corrao, Nicholas Corozzo, Robert Bisaccia and Daniel Marino.

Appeals for new trials normally take place after the defendant has been sentenced. However, John Gotti was no normal defendant. A veritable dream team of lawyers took up his cause a day before sentencing was to take place. The team of attorneys, in addition to Krieger, Cardinale, Mitchell and Cutler, included William M. Kunstler and Ronald L. Kuby. The group was requesting a delay in the sentencing and a motion to set aside the verdict due to affidavits from two jurors who came forward to claim the conviction verdict was unfair. One juror, the last one to be removed, stated she was replaced because she claimed she saw FBI Agent George Gabriel, while sitting at the prosecution table, "flash" a signal to fellow agent Louis Schiliro on the witness stand. The other juror was alleged to have been concerned about his wife's health, but was kept on the jury and pressured into a quick verdict. Judge Glasser rejected the appeal.

On April 2, 1992, at the end of an intensely publicized trial in Federal District Court, The jury took only a day and a half to find John Gotti guilty of all 13 counts against him, including a racketeering charge that cited him for five murders, and related charges of murder, conspiracy, gambling, and obstruction of justice and tax fraud.

Frank Locascio was convicted of the racketeering charge, which cited him for one murder, and six related charges that included a murder conspiracy, gambling, obstruction of justice and tax fraud.

On June 23, 1992, John Gotti and Frank Locascio stood before Judge Glasser to receive their sentence. In a court session that took less than 10 minutes, with the lawyers for both sides choosing not to make statements, the judge asked Mr. Gotti if he had anything to say before the sentence was imposed. Gotti, wearing a dark double-breasted suit, white shirt and bright yellow tie flecked with burnt orange, only shook his head in silence. His longtime lawyer, Bruce Cutler, spoke for him, saying simply, "No, your honor."

Judge Glasser, citing Federal sentencing guidelines adopted in 1987, told Gotti that "the guidelines in your case require me to commit you to the custody of the Attorney General for the duration of your life."

Turning to Locascio, the judge asked if he had anything to say. Locascio who was convicted as the Gambino underboss responded by reading a handwritten statement in a spiral notebook.

"First, I would like to say emphatically that I am innocent," Locascio declared in loud, firm voice, denying each charge that was brought against him.

"I am guilty though," he added, "I am guilty of being a good friend of John Gotti. And if there were more men like John Gotti on this earth, we would have a better country."

As hundreds of chanting, flag-waving Gotti supporters protested in front of the Federal courthouse in Brooklyn, Judge I. Leo Glasser sentenced the boss of the Gambino crime family in a courtroom so packed that James M. Fox, the head of the New York office of the F.B.I., was wedged next to Joseph DeCicco, a reputed Gambino associate.

Gotti's trial lawyer, Albert J. Krieger, said that Gotti patted Locascio on the shoulder after the sentencing and told him, "We have just begun to fight." Mr. Krieger described Gotti's mood as "dignified, strong, resolute" and confident of winning on appeal.

Locascio's trial lawyers, Anthony M. Cardinale and John W. Mitchell, also stressed that the convictions would be appealed.

Gotti will be sent to a maximum security prison, but Federal officials have not said which one.

At 10 A.M., Gotti and Locascio, surrounded by their lawyers and Federal marshals, left the courtroom.

In September 1998, the *New York Daily News* reported that Gotti put out a murder contract on his former consigliere. By now Gravano's book, *Underboss*, had been released, and Gotti was infuriated about comments Sammy related about Locascio, after an incident when the three were in the MCC in 1991. Gotti had belittled Locascio in front of other inmates after he had stolen some oranges and gave one to Gravano before offering one to Gotti. According to Gravano, an emotionally upset Locascio claimed, "The minute I get out, I'm killing this motherfucker."

Meanwhile, outside the courthouse a riot, allegedly organized by John A. "Junior" Gotti, was in full force. An estimated 800 to 1,000 demonstrators, who arrived in 12 chartered buses, began with flag-waving and chanting. When the sentence was announced, violence began. The rioters targeted cars parked in front of the courthouse. Some were turned over, others the crowd jumped upon and shouted, "Free John Gotti!" Eight police officers were injured during the melee and a dozen protestors were arrested.

The Day John Gotti
Got Beat!

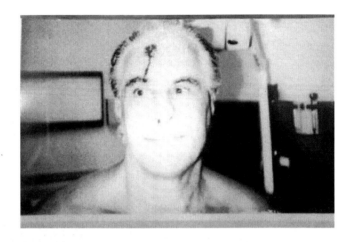

When John Gotti was convicted in June of 1992 and sentenced to multiple life terms in prison the government didn't waste any time in shipping John out to one of the most punitive and restrictive federal prisons in the United States - Marion Federal Penitentiary in Marion, Illinois.

Classified as a "super-max" facility designed to house the most dangerous and incorrigible of offenders, Marion was the place for the worst of the worst. And for a guy like John Gotti, who was the boss of one of the largest and most powerful organized crime families in America Marion seemed like the perfect place befitting a guy of Gotti's stature in the criminal underworld.

Confined to his tiny eight-by-ten jail cell an average of twenty-three hours per day, and with nothing more than a small thirteen-inch black and white television set and a thin mattress atop a concrete slab of a bed to count as luxuries, Gotti was a world away from the personal luxuries and privileges he had enjoyed as Godfather.

But Gotti was still the Boss! Even under the harsh and restrictive conditions of prison, John was in control of himself and his environment. His notoriety and influence transcended prison walls, his supporters said. Other inmates, from murderers to terrorists to common street thugs, gave Gotti a wide berth as he swaggered through the prison corridors. Offending or assaulting the head of a major organized crime family is never a smart move for those interested in good health and prosperity, whether in prison or out on the street!

Who in their right mind would want to mess with Gotti, the "Boss of Bosses" of the Italian Mafia?

The answer to that question turned out to be nobody!

At least not for the first four years of Gotti's prison incarceration.

But on a fateful day in the summer of 1996, during one of those rare moments of "recreation" outside of his tiny cell, Gotti met a bold and violent inmate who dealt the Gotti mystique a harsh blow, and left him with a bloody lip, a puffy face, and a bruised ego.

Walter Johnson, a Philadelphia bank robber and small-time hoodlum, was a violent and incorrigible convict who was sent to Marion.

Johnson, who was an African American, seemed the kind of guy who acted in the moment and didn't really give much thought to any resulting consequences. If he had a problem with another inmate, whether it is a two-bit hoodlum or a Mafia boss, Johnson would handle it. He didn't give two shakes about a guy's reputation, something that John Gotti was soon to find out.

The trouble all started rather innocently enough. Walter Johnson and John Gotti, along with an assortment of other inmates, were enjoying a rare moment of recreation time outside of their jail cells, along an indoor walkway between the cell tiers.

John Gotti, proving that his cockiness and overwhelming sense of self-worth had not been dulled by his years of incarceration, walked towards one end of the walkway. Walter Johnson, apparently minding his own business, happened to cross Gotti's path, and in Gotti's estimation, didn't hop out of the way fast enough or show enough respectful distance.

"Get outta my way you fucking nigger, don't you know who I am?" Gotti allegedly said.

Johnson of course knew exactly who Gotti was, but he didn't much care. Johnson moved enough for Gotti to pass. And the exchange appeared to be over.

But Johnson didn't forget the insult. The very next day when the inmates were again taking a recreation break, Johnson walked up to Gotti and punched him right in the face.

Gotti, taken by surprise, fell to the ground in a heap, with Johnson piling on top of him raining blows. Unable to mount an offense, Gotti was protecting himself with his uplifted hands as the guards dove in and pulled Johnson off of Gotti.

Startled inmates stood in awe and neither helped nor joined in. Gotti, who was bleeding from the lip and mouth, was taken to the prison infirmary; Johnson, after being restrained, was put in solitary confinement.

After Gotti was patched up, it appeared that the whole incident was over.

But John Gotti had other ideas. He wasn't about to suffer the indignity of a jailhouse beating at the hands of a lowly criminal and go quietly into the night. In Gotti's mind, Walter Johnson had committed an unforgivable sin, and he had to pay!

And John Gotti, being an experienced and street smart gangster, knew that every prison tends to have a hierarchy; a group of prisoners that tends to exert more of an influence and reach over the general population than others. And Gotti found that group at Marion in the Aryan Brotherhood, a violent white supremacist-based prison gang that has a well-earned reputation for violence and brutality.

The Aryan Brotherhood was alive and well at Marion. And it didn't take John Gotti long to make contact with one of the ruling members of the gang who was housed in Marion. According to law enforcement intelligence, Gotti offered as much as $100,000 to the gang to murder his attacker.

Gotti's offer was gleefully accepted, and Johnson now had a large target on his back. He was going to find out that you don't assault a high-profile inmate like John Gotti without suffering the consequences!

There was only one problem though. Walter Johnson proved to be an elusive target. Prison authorities, apparently aware of the Gotti/Aryan Brotherhood alliance, kept a watchful and protective eye on Johnson.

He was routinely moved and alternated to various sections of the prison, and the Aryan Brotherhood could never isolate him to make the fatal strike. And, to make matters worse, Johnson was eventually paroled and released from prison. John Gotti and the Aryan Brotherhood struck out!

Not only did Gotti try to get the Aryan Brotherhood to kill Walter Johnson, he eventually hired them to protect him in prison.

Gotti struck a deal with the Aryan Brotherhood to protect him behind bars, but when he reneged, they forced him to "crawl back," a gang snitch told the feds in an interview.

Gotti ultimately wound up paying "large sums of money" to the Brotherhood to ensure his safety in the federal prison according to one of several key prosecution documents.

"Wiseguys on the street like the Teflon Don and all that stuff - it doesn't equate in prison," Aryan Brotherhood turncoat Kevin Roach told the Federal investigators in 2001. "They have to rely on people like the Aryan Brotherhood and the [Mexican Mafia] to protect them . . . in prison."

Kevin Roach was a star witness in the massive federal case against the white supremacist prison gang.

He testified that reputed Brotherhood chief Barry (the Baron) Mills provided Gotti with a bodyguard. In exchange, the Gambino crime boss agreed to arrange for a high-powered attorney to represent Mills in his appeal on a murder conviction in Atlanta, Roach said. In 1994, after Gotti apparently failed to provide the attorney, Mills sent out a "kite" - or secret inter-prison message - saying he "wanted all of the Aryan Brotherhood to know that they were retracting their protection of Gotti," according to an FBI report.

"Mills wanted Gotti to learn a lesson. Sooner or later, Gotti would be assaulted and would have to crawl back to the Aryan Brotherhood," the report said.

Roach told investigators that "Mills laughed and said he knew Gotti was going to end up having to crawl back to us," a Bureau of Prisons report reveals. Gotti started paying "large sums of money to the Aryan Brotherhood on a yearly basis," according to federal documents. Gotti later offered the Brotherhood a contract to kill Johnson, Roach said.

"This information is coming from government snitches and its total fabrication," said Mark Fleming, one of Mills' attorneys. "No money from Gotti ever showed up on any of the defendants' accounts.

Gotti's Final Years

Victoria and John during an unsupervised visit

John Gotti had been in prison less than a year before the government began investigating his son. Although not a true junior to his father, he still bore the nickname.

In March 1993, a grand jury was probing Junior's role in the Gambino Family hierarchy. The younger Gotti, a power weight lifter, met with his crew on Wednesday nights at the Our Friends

Social Club in South Ozone Park, Queens. During the investigation, about twelve gang members were subpoenaed. One of those called was Carmine Agnello, who was married to Junior's sister, author Victoria.

Agnello, who ran a scrap metal operation in Queens, claimed that "scar tissue near his brain has dulled his powers of recall so badly the feds might as well subpoena one of his rusted-out clunkers for all the help he would provide." While seemingly humorous, Agnello's memory problems were actually documented in sealed court papers filed with Judge Nickerson, who presided over the Giacalone RICO trial.

In August 1996, the HBO movie *Gotti* aired. Gotti was played by actor Armand Ansante while two future *Sopranos* stars had key roles; Vincent Pastore played Gotti sidekick Angelo Ruggiero and Tony Sirico was Gene Gotti. While Ansante made an excellent Gotti, little about the film was factually correct. The producers were set on portraying Gotti as a hero, with Sammy Gravano, played by William Forsythe, as the villain. They even had Gravano avenging the killing of Frank Gotti by shooting the John Favara character to death. Gotti, in his fourth year at Marion at the time, was not permitted to view the film.

During the mid-1990s many stories made the news regarding Gotti in prison. The fact that the mob boss was jailed for life did little to keep him, his family or his followers out of the newspapers and public eye. These stories discussed how many hours Gotti was in lockdown each day. Some reporters claimed he was allowed out of his cell for only one hour each day. Other reports had him being transferred to the new "super security" federal prison in Florence, Colorado. One story had Gotti being beaten to a bloody pulp after using a racial slur around another prisoner. A *New York Times* article in October 1996 said at a recent meeting of the Commission, members decided that, since Gotti had no chance of ever receiving a parole, he was about to "abdicate" his leadership of the Gambino Family. It was difficult to determine how much truth there was to these stories, because Bruce Cutler, now relegated to the role of mouthpiece for the Gotti family, denied every rumor and report.

Gotti's continued leadership of the Gambino Crime Family was the hot topic of discussion in the late fall of 1996. On November 24, Jerry Capeci, in his

New York Daily News role, reported that his sources had confirmed that, "Under pressure from the Commission," Gotti was ready to relinquish control of the family. Supposedly, Junior Gotti was serving as acting boss of the family, with Peter Gotti, John "Jackie Nose" D'Amico and Nicholas Corozzo a Gotti co-defendant in the Giacalone trial), serving as advisors. Capeci's sources stated that the new Gambino leader was to be Corozzo.

If Corozzo did indeed ascend to the throne of the Gambino Family it was a short reign. On December 18, Corozzo was indicted on racketeering charges in Florida that included attempted murder, loansharking and arson. Represented by his nephew, Joseph Corozzo, Jr., who would later represent Gotti, Nicholas "Little Nicky" Corozzo was held without bail. In August 1997, Nicholas Corozzo pled guilty to federal racketeering charges in Florida; he received a term of five to ten years. Later that year, he again pled guilty in a Brooklyn courtroom to charges of racketeering and bribing a jail guard.

While Gotti continued to waste away in prison, his one-time underboss Sammy Gravano was living the high life. Fresh from prison, after testifying and ending the three-trial win streak Gotti had held against law enforcement, the man who had admitted to taking part in 19 murders had co-authored a book. He also had a movie deal in the works. At the same time relatives of Gravano's victims were preparing to sue him in a civil action, while a New York State victims' rights attorney was looking to separate Gravano from his profits under the "Son of Sam" law. Years later, a judge would rule against the victim's families, claiming the law was a state statute and Gravano had been convicted of federal crimes. In July 1997, Gravano would make his last appearance as a government witness by testifying against Genovese Family boss Vincent "the Chin" Gigante. Gravano's testimony helped convict the mob boss, known as the "Oddfather," who for years feigned insanity as a means of avoiding prosecution.

Vincent (Chin) Gigante in custody

In April 1997 Judge Glasser shot down Gotti's last bid for a new trial. It was the fourth time that Glasser denied the Dapper Don's request. John Gotti was destined to die behind bars.

The Years Were Not Kind

The last half of the 1990s was not good ones for the former "Teflon Don" or for his family. The government was in hot pursuit of Junior and they watched his every move. In March 1997, State Organized Crime Task Force investigators raided Junior's social club in Queens and seized over $350,000 in cash, which the officers suspected came from illegal operations. Junior gave them the implausible story that it was money he received from his 1990 wedding to Kimberly Albanese.

Even John Gotti's old social club, the Ravenite, couldn't escape the law. In October 1997, U. S. Marshals seized the building and threw out whoever was in the club. Later sold, the building was refurbished and the once infamous clubhouse was turned into a boutique.

In January 1998, Junior was arrested along with 39 others, in a massive federal indictment that charged him with a plethora of crimes, from the mob basics, loansharking and extortion, to a modern day telecommunications scam. Adding insult to injury – at least in the view of the Gotti family – was a June 2 indictment charging Junior in a November 1996 robbery of a drug dealer, in which he allegedly stole two kilos of cocaine, four guns and $4,000 in cash. This time Junior's mother came to his defense. In a rare interview, Victoria Gotti called the *New York Daily News* and stated sarcastically, "He doesn't have enough money, so he gets involved with drugs? Please! Can't they come up with something better than that? ...I wish every mother in America had a son like mine."

Junior's indictment and subsequent legal woes proved to be a family affair, with mom, dad and his two sisters playing key roles. Prosecutors first approached young Gotti with a deal, worked through Gravano nemesis Ronald Kuby, who was representing one of Junior's co-defendants. The deal was contingent upon all the defendants accepting it. Gotti family legal stalwarts – Cutler and Shargel – initially represented Junior, but later, attorney Sarita Kedia emerged as his main counsel.

Junior nixed the prosecution's first deal, but with one of his co-defendants becoming a government witness, the acting boss of the Gambino Family was having second thoughts. In early July 1998, Federal Judge Barrington Parker set a January 1999 trial date.

Junior had already been in jail for over five months and his lawyers were determined to get bail for him. This long legal battle was finally resolved, and on October 1, Junior was allowed to return home. The Gottis had to come up with a $10 million dollar bail, the bulk of which came from Victoria and her husband Carmine Agnello's Old Westbury, Long Island mansion. The balance was provided by sister Angel and 25 other family members and friends.

There were other conditions that had to be met as well, as Junior was whisked away to his Mill Neck, Long Island home in Victoria's Mercedes. The *New York Daily News* reported:

"He will wear an ankle bracelet and be unable to leave his home under almost any conditions. The only exception is for legal strategy meetings with his co-defendants at lawyers' offices, and that would have to be approved by White Plains Federal Judge Barrington Parker.

"FBI agents will make random searches of his home, and approved visitors – with the exception of immediate family members – will be kept in one monitored room.

"Gotti's home phone will be tapped, and he won't be allowed to use either a fax machine or cell phone, but he'll have a second phone for private talks with attorneys. Still, he'll have access to his swimming pool and tennis courts."

The government prosecutors had frozen Junior's properties, causing him to claim that he was on the brink of insolvency. Outside the Federal Courthouse in White Plains, New York, Junior railed at reporters, "Who's the racketeers?"

Part of the bail agreement was that Junior had to pay for a 24-hour private security firm to monitor his every move. The cost of the security was $21,000 a month. Due to the government's seizures, by early December Junior was screaming poverty. This, along with new charges being generated by the government, was beginning to wear the 34-year-old Gotti down.

As Junior began to give more consideration to a new plea deal from the government, he started to receive pressure from both his mother and father to go to trial. Just after Christmas, Junior rejected the government's latest deal. By early January of 1999, three key defendants, including John D'Amico, had accepted plea agreements. With the additional charges the prosecutors were putting together, the January trial date was pushed back to April 6. By mid-March, only Junior and one other Gambino associate were left to stand trial, out of the 40 men originally indicted. On April 1, Junior told Judge Parker he could no longer afford the 24-hour security and asked to be sent back to jail.

On April 6, the day jury selection was to begin, Junior shocked his family and friends by accepting a government offer to serve 77 months for extortion, loansharking, gambling, mortgage fraud and tax evasion. In addition, he forfeited $1.5 million in cash and property. On October 18, 1999, over six months after pleading guilty, John A. "Junior" Gotti entered a medium-security federal prison in Ray Brook, New York, 300 miles from home and family.

In the middle of Junior's long legal wrangling, it was suddenly announced that his father had been transferred to the United States Medical Center for Federal Prisoners in Springfield, Missouri. John Gotti had been diagnosed with throat cancer.

Acting as spokesperson for the family, Cutler stated, "Doctors found a tumor near his tonsils and lymph nodes at the back of Gotti's throat. It's serious. It's life-threatening."

In late September 1998, The Dapper Don was operated on. Doctors removed a cancerous tumor, but were optimistic that a full recovery would take place.

More Family Woes

The next family member to fall to law enforcement was Carmine Agnello. On one of her visits to see her father in Marion prison, Victoria listened during the taped session as John Gotti asked, "So what's the story with Carmine? Does he get in the backseat of the car and think someone has stolen the steering wheel?" This was only one of the demeaning remarks that showed the disrespect Papa Gotti had for his son-in-law. The events of January 2000 would have little effect in changing Gotti's perception of Agnello.

In April 1999, undercover police from the Auto Crimes Division in Queens set up an undercover sting operation in the Willets Point section near Shea Stadium. The sting was set up to catch thieves selling stolen auto parts.

Before the month was out in walked Agnello to inform the undercover operators that they would have to sell him parts at half price in order to stay in business. Rebuked by the officers, Agnello twice attempted to burn down the operation to make his point. He was later indicted and charged with coercion, conspiracy, grand larceny and arson, not to mention restraint of trade and enterprise corruption.

On January 25, 2000, Agnello was taken into custody and held on $10 million dollars bail, prompting his then attorney, Marvyn Kornberg, to utter his famous line, "That's not bail, it's a telephone number." Three Agnello associates were also indicted. Queens' prosecutors moved quickly to freeze Agnello's assets, and they even took the unusual step of having police follow Victoria and surround an ATM machine at a Pathmark store to keep her from withdrawing money from the family accounts.

It seems as though, of all the Gotti family members, the stunningly attractive Victoria is the most intelligent, as well as the most talented and successful. The author of several best-selling novels, Victoria had handled the majority of the arrangements to bail out brother Junior a year earlier, only to see him sent away for six-plus years. Now she was looking at the prospect of seeing her husband incarcerated for a lengthy prison term.

After hearings, the bail was reduced so that Victoria, using $125,000 from a book advance, could free her husband with the help of friends and family. Agnello's return to his Old Westbury mansion would be short, but certainly not sweet. Information from the investigation alleged that Agnello was having an affair with one of his employees. Despite initial denials by both himself and his wife, the following year Victoria would divorce Agnello, ending 15 years of marriage to the hot-headed 38 year-old mobster.

Meanwhile, on March 7, 2000, Agnello was arrested again. Named in a sweeping federal indictment, FBI agents awakened Agnello one morning and hauled him into a Brooklyn Federal Courthouse where he was charged and held without bail. This time Victoria was unsuccessful in her attempts to bail him out. He remains in jail as of this writing awaiting trial.

The one offspring who seemed to keep a low profile was Peter Gotti, the youngest of the children. In early April 2001, Peter was pulled over at a Rego Park, Queens police sobriety check point, where he was arrested for driving without a license.

After spending the night in jail, he was fined $80. The beefy 26 year-old had a long record of traffic violations, and he'd had his license suspended or revoked on four separate occasions. In 1994, he'd allegedly attacked a policeman who was in the act of issuing him a traffic citation.

In the years since John Gotti's 1992 imprisonment, if there has been anything to make the former Teflon Don happy, it would had to have been the arrest of his former underboss Sammy "the Bull" Gravano. On February 24, 2000, Gravano, his wife and two children were arrested in Arizona for their participation in a statewide drug ring that distributed the new designer drug, Ecstasy.

A subsequent indictment was issued against Gravano and his son Gerard in New York, charging them with conspiring with Israeli mobsters to distribute Ecstasy. As a June 4, 2001 trial date approached, Gravano and son agreed to plead guilty. On May 25, Gravano appeared in the same Brooklyn Federal Courthouse where he had testified against John Gotti. While the families of Gravano's murder victims listened, Sammy told Judge Allyn Ross, "I loaned money to people" who purchased Ecstasy. Gravano was scheduled to be sentenced in September 2001. That same month Gravano goes on trial in Arizona. It's unlikely that within the next fifteen years, the Mafia's most celebrated "rat" will be a free man.

Finally, on April 18, 2001 the *New York Daily News* announced that John Gotti "has taken a turn for the worse." They reported that the cancer doctors thought had gone away had returned, and now the Dapper Don was suffering from its advanced stages and was expected to last just two months. Gotti's lawyer, Joseph Corozzo, told reporters that John was putting up a brave front. "He's forced to be in a wheelchair," the attorney stated, but emphasized that Gotti "insists on getting about on his own without assistance. John is defiant to the end."

The following week the *New York Post* reported that the medical facility, the Bureau of Prisons hospital in Springfield, Missouri, had relaxed its regulation and Gotti was allowed to have limited contact with family members. They stated that "he is allowed to hug his wife, his two daughters, his son, and other relatives while prison videotape rolls."

Week from chemotherapy treatments, Gotti was receiving nutrition and medication through intravenous tubes. When not visiting with family members Gotti still spent most of his time in solitary confinement.

On April 25, 2001, Junior Gotti was transferred from Ray Brook prison to the Atlanta Federal Penitentiary, in the hope that he would testify at the trial of Steve Kaplan, an alleged Gambino Family associate. Kaplan and several others were on trial in federal court in Atlanta on racketeering conspiracy charges, which included loansharking, prostitution, illegal ties to organized crime, credit card fraud and police corruption. The prosecution charged that Kaplan paid Junior Gotti protection money from his high class Gold Club, a popular Atlanta strip club that drew big names athletes.

On May 17, in a private hearing in the judge's chambers, Gotti was asked four questions, to which Junior invoked his Fifth Amendment right not to answer. He was then returned to 23-hour lockdown in the Atlanta prison.

The newspapers reported that Gotti would "likely be returned to prison in upstate New York within days." However, nearly a month later, when it was reported that his father was near death, Junior was still en route back to Ray Brook.

The *New York Daily News* reported on June 13, 2001 that John Gotti had lost so much weight that chemotherapy treatments were discontinued. The following day, it was reported that the former Teflon Don was suffering from pneumonia and that shunts which helped deliver medicine into his body had developed infections around them. An unnamed source said, "It's a matter of weeks." The Gotti family was upset because they were unable to speak with Junior while he was still in transit. Although he was flown to Atlanta in a trip that took a total of five hours, the government was giving him the "scenic route" back, placing him on a prison bus that had stops in three different states along the way.

Gotti's Final Days

It was announced in the New York Daily News that Gotti had taken a turn for the worse. He was now suffering from the advanced stages and was not expected to live past two months. Although he was insistent on getting around with little assistance, he was forced to be in a wheelchair. He was extremely weak from the chemotherapy treatments and his appetite had waned. The prison hospital had to eventually feed him through intravenous tubes.

He was finally allowed to have limited contact with family members. A hug for his wife and children was now permitted. After each visit Gotti would be taken back to his solitary confinement.

By June 13, 2001 he had lost too much weight and the chemotherapy was stopped. The next day it was apparent that he was suffering from pneumonia. It seemed as though he was falling apart. Even the shunts that delivered pain medication had developed infections. It looked as though the end was near. But being the strong man he was, he wouldn't give the disease the satisfaction and held on for another year.

On June 10, 2002, John finally passed away and was finally allowed to come home to New York. Still he was met with the indignity of being turned away from his parish church. It's seems odd how the Catholic church can turn a blind eye and allow a child molesting priest who commits suicide, a Catholic burial but yet deny John Gotti.

He finally received a funeral at a Queens church and was laid to rest next to his son at St. John's Cemetery.

As his daughter, Victoria once said, he is the last of the Mohicans

Part Four
Farewell to a King

This according to sources is the private jet used to transport John's body to Republic Airport in Farmingdale, New York. If you look closely through the window you can see workers removing his body.

His body was then taken to Papavero Funeral Home in Maspeth, New York. Many people paid tribute to John in true Mafia Style....Flowers lots of flowers.

A framed picture of a smiling, tanned Gotti stood by the closed gold coffin. Gotti had worn a prison jumpsuit the last 10 years in the federal penitentiary in Marion, Ill. In death, he was laid out in a blue suit and blue tie.

New York City police officers set up barricades to keep traffic away from the funeral home in the residential working class neighborhood in Queens and allowed in only those who lived on the street -- and of course the dozens of flower trucks.

A steady stream of giant flower arrangements, often taking two men to carry, arrived in the funeral home in the shapes of playing cars, boxing gloves, race horses, the New York Yankees emblem, a cigar, a martini with real olives and an eight-foot arrangement of exotic flowers.

"Do not stand at my grave and weep; I am not there, I do not sleep. ... Do not stand at my grave and cry, I am not there, I did not die," prayer cards said.

Many who made their way to the Papavero Funeral Home were left standing outside in the rain because there was no room inside.

Several of Gotti's relatives were not there.

His brother, Gene, serving a 50-year sentence for heroin trafficking and his son, John A. "Junior," serving a 6-year sentence for racketeering and gambling, did not ask for permission from prison officials to attend the wake, according to Gotti's lawyer.

"Like John Gotti never asked for anything from the government, neither will his son," Bruce Cutler said of the decision of Gotti's son not to attend the final rites of this father.

Another Gotti who did not attend the wake was Gotti's brother Peter who is being held without bail after he and 16 members of the Gambino crime family were indicted for racketeering, extortion, wire-fraud, loan sharking, operating illegal gambling businesses, money laundering and witness tampering.

In fact, many members of the faded Gambino crime family are either in jail, dead or on parole and restricted from associating with "known criminals."

However, members of the Bonanno, Colombo and Lucchese crime families of New York City are expected to send representatives.

It was not expected that members of the Genovese crime family would pay their respects to Gotti because none of them attended John A. "Junior" Gotti's wedding in 1990.

Many believe the Genovese crime family has replaced the Gambino crime family as the most powerful crime organization in the country.

Traditionally, members of law enforcement observe family events of organized crime members to get a clue to "who is kissing whom" because the person being "respected" the most by being kissed on the cheek is rising to the top of the mob family.

However, some members of organized crime did not show up at Gotti's wake as a sign of "disrespect."

Many have blamed Gotti's attraction to the limelight as the undoing of the Gambino crime family because it brought too much attention to their activities.

The Gotti family had asked the Roman Catholic Church to say a funeral Mass for Gotti but the family was refused by the Diocese of Brooklyn.

According to Gotti associates, the hearse of the 61-year-old New York City native was drive by the modest two-story Gotti home in Howard Beach and by his headquarters at the Bergin Hunt and Fish Club before taking the body to the cemetery.

Gotti had expressed the desire to be buried alongside his son in St. John's Cemetery in Middle Village where a Who's Who of mobsters are buried including Carlo Gambino, Carmine Galante, Joseph Profaci, Vito Genovese, Charles "Lucky" Luciano and Aniello Dellacroce.

The Brooklyn Diocese did allow Gotti to be interred in the Gotti family mausoleum in St. John's Cemetery where his son, Frank, was interred.

A priest said prayers at the burial at the mausoleum.

The church has said that a Mass for the Dead can be celebrated for Gotti after he is interred.

Gotti was survived by his wife Victoria, their four children and four brothers: Gene, Vincent, Peter and Richard.

These photos are of the pallbearers carrying his casket to the hearse to be taken to St. John's Cemetery which is also in Queens.

The procession to the cemetery is unbelievable

The people of New York loved John Gotti.

Twilight of the Gotti Gangsters

It was not a typical mob case. It hopped on the public radar screen with the testimony of popular actor Steven Seagal. An amazing story followed that showed how the mob tried to get a foothold in the American film industry.

Steven Seagal, 50, had a partner named Julius Nasso, who prosecutors claim was a Gambino crime family associate. They had caught Nasso on tape agreeing to force Seagal to pay $150,000 to the crime family for every film Seagal made. This agreement, valued at some $3 million, was to be executed by Anthony "Sonny" Ciccone who tried to extort the money from Seagal at a restaurant.

Seagal testified that Ciccone said, "Look at me when I talk to you. We are proud people. Work with Jules and we'll split the pie." The government had the restaurant bugged and the mobsters commented on how frightened Seagal appeared to be after they delivered their extortion threat.

After the meeting, Seagal said that his former partner told him, "If you would have said the wrong thing, they would have killed you"

On March 18, 2003, Peter Gotti, 63, brother of the late crime czar John Gotti, was found guilty of racketeering and taking control of the Gambino crime enterprise. Along with Gotti were six co-defendants including the men who had tried to extort money from Seagal.

Peter Gotti

"They got me," Peter Gotti said afterwards. "It's easy to convict a Gotti. All you have to have is the name."

The Associated Press reported that Gotti "was the star defendant in the far-reaching mob case alleging a campaign of extortion stretching from the city's waterfront to Hollywood. Prosecutors accused him of pocketing thousands of dollars from various schemes. In addition to racketeering, Gotti also was found guilty of conspiracy and multiple counts of money laundering."

Two other Gotti family members were also convicted of racketeering, Richard V. Gotti, another brother of John Gotti, and Richard G. Gotti, a nephew of the late crime boss.

Court TV reported, "On Gotti's watch, a violent Gambino crew used threats to assume control of local chapters of the International Longshoremen's Association. The family then rigged union elections and secured the award of a lucrative union health service contract for a mob-controlled company.

"During a six-week trial, prosecutors presented a series of surveillance photos and tapes of known gangsters paying homage and cash to Gotti," proving that Peter Gotti was "not only a mobster, but a mob leader."

Newsday reported that "despite lacking evidence showing the reputed mob boss Peter Gotti actually took money from anyone, federal prosecutors were able to connect enough dots between bits of circumstantial evidence to convict him of money laundering and racketeering."

Things are not looking good these days for the Gotti dynasty's hold on the Gambino crime family. First, the notorious John Gotti was convicted. Then his son, John Gotti, known as "Junior," was also convicted and jailed. And now Peter and his brother Richard and nephew will also go to jail. It cannot be denied that the Gotti mobster line is in its twilight.

The Next Generation: Victoria

Victoria Gotti

Victoria Gotti is not the typical mob princess. She is an attractive woman, mother of three teenage boys, author of several books and the subject of a new reality show. She has leveraged her father's mob boss career into a profitable business.

Not only that American Media has made her editor-in chief of a new celebrity lifestyle magazine called *Red Carpet.*

Blunt, outspoken and very tough, she has a lot of her father's talents, but, unlike John Gotti, used in legitimate pursuits.

The reviews of her latest entrepreneurial venture have been mixed. "Growing up Gotti," says the *New York Times,* "is a one-joke novelty item, but it is at times quite funny and Ms. Gotti is an oddly compelling figure...raising three loutish teenage boys on a sprawling, deliciously vulgar Long Island estate."

``Growing up with my father, I was very sheltered," she told BostonHerald.com. ``My father was very, very strict with us. He wouldn't allow anyone to curse in front of any women. He was old-fashioned. I had a midnight curfew until I got married. I was very protected."

"So are her sons, and though Gotti knows celebrity can wreak havoc on even the most level-headed, she's not worried. Plus, the boys don't want to be famous. Carmine is going to Harvard to become a criminal attorney, John wants to be a writer and Frank wants to be a chef," she said.

Comparisons to Carmella Soprano are inevitable, but she told the Associated Press that she never watches the popular show.

"I just find it offensive," she said. "Forget the mob stuff, it's the way the women walk around cracking gum and talking about trivial nonsense. Italian women are stunning and cultured, and they're smart. It doesn't portray them like that."

She maintains that she does not stay in touch with her brother John Jr. who is chronically in trouble with the feds. It was bad enough to have an ex-husband, Carmine Agnello, whose racketeering landed him in jail for a long stretch. She doesn't' need role models like those with three growing sons.

The Next Generation: John Jr.

John A. Gotti, known as "Junior," went on trial August 8, 2005, for the alleged 1992 kidnapping of talk show host Curtis Sliwa, founder of the Guardian Angels, to stop him from criticizing the Gotti family. The Guardian Angels was a crime-fighting group that made citizen arrests.

Junior's attorneys have claimed that Junior had left the world of organized crime out of a concern for his children.

Federal prosecutors said that Junior "ordered his thugs" to kidnap Sliwa because he was enraged at Sliwa's criticism of organized crime. According to CNN, Sliwa was attacked "by bat-wielding young men, leaving him with a broken hand and an injured scalp." Two months later, Sliwa was abducted and shot twice while in a cab, and was hospitalized for internal injuries and leg wounds. He "saved himself only by leaping out an open window," the AP reported.

"The cab was intended to be a hearse," U.S. Attorney David Kelley told reporters at a news conference.

The feds intended to prove that Junior Gotti is also involved in traditional mob crimes such as loansharking and extortion.

John Gotti Jr

Forty-year-old John Gotti Jr., who was about to be released from prison in September, 2004, for racketeering, faced a federal indictment along with three other members of the Gambino crime family.

The indictment, unsealed on July 22, 2004, involved a number of major crimes, including kidnapping, murder, and attempted murder, conspiracy to commit securities fraud, illegal gambling and fraud.

The problem was there in a year's time, there were three mistrials. The feds do not plan to try John "Junior" Gotti a fourth time. Curtis Sliwa intends to file a civil suit.

Gotti says that he plans to leave New York and relocate in the Midwest. Is this the end of the Gotti crime epic? Don't count on it.

Jack Falcone

Retired FBI agent, Joaquin Garcia infiltrated the Gambino crime family under the alias of Jack Falcone beginning in 2002. Greg DePalma, the Gambino family capo, offered Garcia the position of Made Man.

However, the FBI investigation ceased in 2005 when Garcia's cover was in danger of being blown.

But, with sufficient evidence to convict DePalma and several other high-ranking members, DePalma was arrested and convicted to twelve years in federal prison thanks in large part to Garcia's efforts.

Operation Old Bridge

On Thursday, February 7, 2008, an indictment and four-year-long FBI investigation known as Operation Old Bridge was issued, leading to 54 people affiliated with the Gambino crime family being arrested that very day in New York City and its northern suburbs, New Jersey and Long Island.

A federal grand jury later that day accused 62 people of having ties to the Gambino crime family and offenses such as murders, conspiracy, drug trafficking, robberies, extortion and other crimes were included in the indictment. By the end of the week, more than 80 people were indicted in the Eastern District of New York.

The case is now referred to as United States of America v. Agate et al. It was assigned to Judge Nicholas Garaufis. The FBI was able to collect the needed information through informant Joseph Vollero, the owner of a truck company on Staten Island, who secretly recorded several conversations between him and members of the Gambino family about three years prior to when the indictment was handed out.

Among the arrested were the current Gambino crime family leaders John "Jackie Nose" D'Amico, Joseph "Jo Jo" Corozzo and Domenico "Italian Dom" Cefalu, including Gambino family caporegime Leonard "Lenny" DiMaria, Francesco "Frank" Cali, Thomas "Tommy Sneakers" Cacciopoli.

However, recognized captain and co-acting boss Nicholas "Little Nick" Corozzo, one of the main indicted in the case, fled his home on Long Island, acting on prior knowledge, and was considered a fugitive by US law enforcement until his arrest before turning himself in on May 29, 2008 after almost four months on the run.

The federal operation broke up a growing alliance between the Gambinos and the Sicilian Mafia, who wanted to get further into the drug trade. One of those arrested in the raids in the US was Frank Cali, a captain in the Gambino family. He is allegedly the "ambassador" in the US for the Inzerillo crime family.

The Gambino Family today

From 2005 to 2008, federal authorities successfully prosecuted the Gambino administration, several capos, and many soldiers and associates. Since both federal and New York State authorities rounded up the entire Gambino family hierarchy in early 2008, there is an apparent power-vacuum in the Gambino family.

Many speculate the new acting boss is the legendary Castellano-loyalist Daniel "Danny" Marino of the Queens faction of the family. Fresh out of jail, Carmine Agnello is also being watched very closely.

A March 2009 article in the New York Post stated that a three-man panel of street bosses Daniel "Danny" Marino, John Gambino and Bartolomeo "Bobby" Vernace was running the Gambino family while the administration members were in prison. The article also stated that the family included of approximately 260 "made" members. Both street boss Jackie D'Amico and acting underboss Domenico Cefalu had finished serving prison terms on November 3, 2009, but D'Amico was kept in custody and pled guilty to new charges that will keep him in prison for up to three more years.

In 2009, former National Basketball Association (NBA) referee Tim Donaghy said that Gambino associate James Battista used Donaghy's knowledge of NBA games to pick winners in illegal sports gambling.

Today the Gambino family still controls the piers in Brooklyn and Staten Island through infiltrating labor unions.

A pair of indictments in 2009 and 2010, respectively, shows the family is still very active in New York City.

On November 18, 2009, the NYPD arrested 22 members and associates of the Lucchese and Gambino crime families as part of "Operation Pure Luck". The raid was a result of cases involving loan sharking and sports gambling on Staten Island.

There were also charges of bribing New York City court officers and Sanitation Department officials.

On April 20, 2010, Gambino capo Daniel Marino and thirteen other members/associates were arrested and indicted for numerous criminal activities. In additions to the racketeering charges, the fourteen defendants were charged with murder, sex trafficking, sex trafficking of a minor, jury tampering, extortion, assault, wire fraud, narcotics trafficking, loan-sharking and gambling.

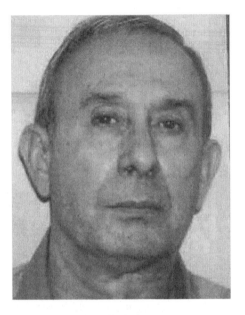

Domenico Cefalù

For four years it is said that Domenico Cefalù took control of the Gambino's, officially. In 1991 just before John Gotti was put away, he made Cefalù a made member of the family and 20 years later he would go on to run it.

Cefalù was a member of the Sicilian "Zip" crew headed by captain Pasquale Conte and based in Queens and Brooklyn.

In 1992, a New York grand jury summoned Cefalù to testify in an investigation of Pasquale Conte. After answering a few questions, Cefalù refused to testify. The judge sentenced Cefalù to 18 months in jail for civil contempt.

On February 23, 1993, Cefalù was summoned to testify in Conte's trial, but again refused. On February 6, 1994, Cefalù was released from jail. However on February 6, 1994, Cefalù was indicted on criminal contempt for refusing to testify at Conte's trial. In 1996, convicted of criminal contempt, the court sentenced Cefalù to 33 months in prison.

In 2005, Cefalù was named family underboss by street boss and former ally of John Gotti, John D'Amico. One of his main responsibilities was overseeing the Sicilian faction of the Gambino family.

On February 7, 2008, Cefalù was indicted on multiple charges of racketeering conspiracy and extortion as part of the Operation Old Bridge investigation of the Gambino family. The extortion charges came from the trucking industry, which hauls away dirt excavated from construction projects. Cefalù accepted a plea agreement from the prosecution in exchange for a guilty plea that could have resulted in his spending up to three years in prison. Cefalù was sentenced to 33 months in prison. On November 3, 2009, Cefalù was released from federal prison. Cefalù currently resides in Brooklyn and lives with his mother. His legitimate employment is as a salesman for a bakery.

In July 2011, Cefalù became the official boss of the Gambino crime family. His ascension was seen as a return to the old-fashion way of running a Mafia family. He replaced Peter Gotti, who had been sentenced to life imprisonment in 2002 while a series of acting bosses and ruling panels was used to run the family. This also marked the end of the John Gotti era of the Gambino family. Gotti had been in charge of the Gambino family since 1986 and when imprisoned used several close criminal associates and blood relatives to run the Gambino family before and after his death. Cefalù is the first person since Gotti went to prison to lead the family who was not a Gotti ally.

In 2013 The Gambino crime family is set to named Francesco "Franky Boy" Cali as its new godfather.

Francesco "Franky Boy" Cali

Cali — a native New Yorker who traces his roots firmly to Sicily — was secretly anointed as the head of the nation's largest La Cosa Nostra organization.

The sources say Cali's ascent from underboss was imminent and will put him in complete control of the Mafia family that has 750 members and associates.

A top New York City law enforcement source said the Gambino capos continue to look up to Cali, because of his old-school approach to running a massive crime family, his adherence to traditional Mafia values, personal family ties that stretch across the Atlantic to Italy and his insistence that members maintain a low profile.

The latter continues a break with the flashy, headline-grabbing era marked by Gotti, whose visage once graced the cover of Time magazine.

Sources said former boss, Domenico "Greaseball" Cefalu, 76, was a native Sicilian with a long history of heroin smuggling and several stints in prison. He was stepping aside to allow his younger protégé to take the reins of the family's lucrative gambling, loansharking and construction rackets.

"The family believes Cali is more dynamic and that Cefalu has become too laid back . . . and that's not what a money making organization wants," another law enforcement source said.

Cali got his start in the mob by running a fruit store on 18th Avenue in Brooklyn called Arcobaleno, which means "rainbow" in Italian. The feds say it doubled as a front for criminal activities.

His parents immigrated to Brooklyn from Palermo, Italy. He eventually married into mob royalty when he wed the daughter of one of the Inzerillos, who are known as one of the Mafia powerhouses in Italy.

He is also a nephew of John and Joseph Gambino, who are influential hoods connected to the famous "Pizza Connection" drug trafficking case of the 1980s.

Cali made his bones under the Gottis while operating in Manhattan, Brooklyn and New Jersey.

According to the FBI, he officially became the Gambino "ambassador to the Sicilian Mafia" and a rising star when Gotti and Salvatore "Sammy Bull" Gravano roamed the city, ruling rackets and murdering dozens of people.

In 2008, Cali and scores of other hoods were arrested in a massive drug and racketeering investigation dubbed "Operation Old Bridge" that centered on extortion of a Staten Island trucking executive who became an FBI wire-wearing informant.

The case also involved planned NASCAR races on the island. Cali pleaded guilty to racketeering charges and spent a year in jail.

"The Gambinos like Cali because of his low-key profile and old-school values," a law enforcement source said. "The family wants to keep things that way."

But the mob has remained strong in traditional money-making operations involving gambling, loansharking and prostitution, law enforcement authorities say.

Sammy "The Bull" Gravano

In return for his testimony, Gravano was given a five year sentence, with four years credited for time already served. In the end, he served only one year for the same crimes that left John Gotti imprisoned for life. In 1994, he was released and he and his family entered witness protection. After only a year, the Gravano family left the program, and Gravano began attracting media attention, giving interviews to the likes of Diane Sawyer.

He also wrote a book, titled *Underboss*, which revealed not only the fully extent of many of his crimes, but also John Gotti's. He has since been incarcerated on drug charges, where he remains until at least 2019.

14177004R00129

Made in the USA
Lexington, KY
05 November 2018